Everyday SEL in the Virtual Classroom

Learn specific strategies for implementing social emotional learning (SEL), mindfulness, and well-being in a virtual classroom. This essential new resource from well-being experts Carla Tantillo Philibert and Allison Slade will help you build students' Self-Awareness and Self-Regulation skills, school connectedness, Social Awareness, voice, and agency in remote or hybrid settings.

Appropriate for teachers of all grade levels, as well as for instructional leaders and parents, the book emphasizes the educator's own self-care and emotional intelligence, so you can become more aware of how the environment affects you along with your students. It also offers ideas for planning collaboratively with colleagues and engaging families in the virtual environment. Throughout, the authors share a variety of activities and practices you can implement immediately, along with sample scripts and educator tips.

With the inspiring advice in this book, you'll be able to help create emotionally healthy classrooms and school environments so that all students and educators can thrive, even during the most uncertain times.

Carla Tantillo Philibert is the founder of Mindful Practices, one of the Midwest's leading Social Emotional Learning and well-being organizations. Mindful Practices is a dedicated team who share SEL, mindfulness, and well-being practices with school communities across the globe. Carla and her husband Rob also co-created the SEL check-in platforms Class Catalyst (2nd–12th grade students) and Five to Thrive (early childhood and Learners with Exceptionalities), along with SEL On Demand, a curated catalog of SEL video content.

Allison Slade, Ed.D. is an educational innovator who founded the Namaste Charter School in 2004 in Chicago, IL. It serves 485 students in grades K-8 with the mission to "Educate Children from the Inside Out." After 14 years as a school leader in the city and suburbs, Allison has moved to impact future leaders as the Director of Instructional Leadership at Roosevelt University, where she is redesigning the Principal Preparation program, challenging leaders to become emotionally intelligent educators, and grow emotionally safe and intentional spaces for students.

Also Available from
Carla Tantillo Philibert and Routledge
www.routledge.com/k-12

Everyday SEL in Early Childhood, Second Edition:
Integrating Social Emotional Learning and Mindfulness
into Your Classroom

Everyday SEL in Elementary School, Second Edition:
Integrating Social Emotional Learning and Mindfulness
into Your Classroom

Everyday SEL in Middle School, Second Edition:
Integrating Social Emotional Learning and Mindfulness
into Your Classroom

Everyday SEL in High School, Second Edition:
Integrating Social Emotional Learning and Mindfulness
into Your Classroom

Everyday Self-Care for Educators: Tools and Strategies for Well-Being
With Christopher Soto and Lara Veon

Everyday SEL for Administrators
With Allison Slade

Everyday SEL in the Virtual Classroom

Integrating Social Emotional Learning and Mindfulness Into Your Remote and Hybrid Settings

Carla Tantillo Philibert and Allison Slade

Routledge
Taylor & Francis Group

NEW YORK AND LONDON

Cover image: © Getty Images

First published 2022
by Routledge
605 Third Avenue, New York, NY 10158

and by Routledge
4 Park Square, Milton Park, Abingdon, Oxon, OX14 4RN

Routledge is an imprint of the Taylor & Francis Group, an informa business

© 2022 Carla Tantillo Philibert and Allison Slade

Library of Congress Cataloging-in-Publication Data
Names: Tantillo Philibert, Carla, author. | Slade, Allison, author.
Title: Everyday SEL in the virtual classroom : integrating social emotional
   learning and mindfulness into your remote and hybrid settings /
   Carla Tantillo Philibert, Allison Slade.
Description: New York, NY : Routledge, 2022. | Includes bibliographical
   references.
Identifiers: LCCN 2021046996 (print) | LCCN 2021046997 (ebook) |
   ISBN 9781032023953 (hardback) | ISBN 9781032009032 (paperback) |
   ISBN 9781003183204 (ebook)
Subjects: LCSH: Affective education. | Reflective teaching. | Mindfulness
   (Psychology) | Web-based instruction—Psychological aspects.
Classification: LCC LB1072 .T384 2022 (print) | LCC LB1072 (ebook) |
   DDC 370.15/34—dc23/eng/20211025
LC record available at https://lccn.loc.gov/2021046996
LC ebook record available at https://lccn.loc.gov/2021046997

ISBN: 978-1-032-02395-3 (hbk)
ISBN: 978-1-032-00903-2 (pbk)
ISBN: 978-1-003-18320-4 (ebk)

DOI: 10.4324/9781003183204

Typeset in Palatino
by Apex CoVantage, LLC

Contents

Meet the Authors

Carla Tantillo Philibert founded Mindful Practices in 2006 to share innovative Social Emotional Learning (SEL), mindfulness, and well-being with thousands of students, educators and families nationwide. A certified yoga teacher with a Master's degree in curriculum and instruction, Carla has taught at both the secondary and elementary levels. Carla was a founding teacher and curriculum director of a high school in Chicago's Little Village community, is the co-creator of Hip-HopYoga™ and is the co-founder of the student check-in platforms Class Catalyst and Five to Thrive. Carla is also co-creator of Michigan Public Television's POP Check series. Carla is a highly qualified professional development provider, keynote speaker, and author of *Cooling Down Your Classroom: Using Yoga, Relaxation and Breathing Strategies to Help Students Learn to Keep Their Cool* (2012), *Everyday SEL in Elementary School: Integrating Social-Emotional Learning and Mindfulness Into Your Classroom* (2016), *Everyday SEL in Middle School: Integrating Social-Emotional Learning and Mindfulness Into Your Classroom* (2016), *Everyday SEL in High School: Integrating Social-Emotional Learning and Mindfulness Into Your Classroom* (2017), *Everyday Self-Care for Educators: Tools and Strategies for Well-Being* (2019). Carla is also a contributing author for *Stories of School Yoga: Narratives from the Field* (2019) and *Educating Mindfully: Stories of School Transformation Through Mindfulness* (2020). Carla and her husband Rob have two amazing children, Dottie and Remi, and the family enjoys long adventure walks around Chicago neighborhoods with their black lab.

Allison Slade, Ed.D. is an educational innovator whose disruption of the educational status quo is exemplified in her founding of Namaste Charter School in 2004 in Chicago, IL. Namaste Charter School opened in 2004 and currently serves 485 students in grades K-8 with the mission to "Educate Children from the Inside Out." Namaste uses health, physical fitness, and nutrition as avenues for students to reach their true academic potential. After 14 years as a school leader in the city and suburbs, Dr. Slade has moved to impact future leaders as the Director of Instructional Leadership at Roosevelt University, where she is redesigning the Principal Preparation program to create a new view of the principalship in PK-12 education, specifically integrating and challenging school and teacher leaders to become emotionally intelligent educators, and grow emotionally safe and intentional spaces for students. Over the past 20+ years, Dr. Slade has served as a teacher at the primary level, professional developer, school leader, mentor, and curriculum designer in urban and suburban settings. She is a certified teacher, principal, and superintendent in Chicago and in addition to her work at Roosevelt, she serves as a consultant doing projects that span from teacher and principal professional development to organizational leadership, management, and change. She lives in the suburbs of Chicago with her husband, Michael, her two spirited, dancing daughters, Elise and Gabrielle, and a variety of fish, as various allergies prevent the family from having additional, but desired pets!

The Partnership

Although Carla and Allison have known each other and have collaborated on various projects for decades, they formally partnered up in 2020, as the world of Social Emotional Learning in schools shifted dramatically with the onset of the COVID-19 global pandemic. Never has their shared love, expertise, and passion for emotionally intelligent teaching and leading become more relevant than in a space where education itself has been upended, and the impact and importance of relationship building, mindfulness, and attention to self has taken on new meaning, and a new image. Despite the extensive challenges that come with the world being physically separated and isolated, Carla and Allison see hope and opportunity in the possibility for real and sustaining change in the way SEL and emotionally safe schools and classrooms are finally receiving their long awaited attention in the search for student success across the spectrum.

About Mindful Practices' EdTech SEL Solutions

SEL implementation can be tough—there is never enough *time*! Carla wanted to harness the time-saving power of technology to help educators connect with more kids.

So, she recruited her husband Rob, with his background in all things Internet (user experience, coding, and development and online product development). He immediately said they could digitize practices and strategies to help adults connect one on one with students. Together, they built prototypes, beta tested concepts, and integrated best practices from their research partner, Dr. Kiljoong Kim at Chapin Hall at the University of Chicago, to create evidence-based EdTech SEL solutions for classrooms.

Class Catalyst: SEL Check-In Platform

What: A student-centered platform for connecting students with a caring adult through daily check-ins.

How: A simple check-in to allow students to report on how they are feeling and provide them with guided practices based on their reported state to help them be more present.

When: Once a day for three minutes to practice Self-Awareness and build relational trust with a caring adult.

SEL Focus: Self-Awareness, Self-Regulation, Voice, Agency, Positive Youth Identity, Human Connection, and Relational Trust

Five to Thrive: SEL Check-In Platform for Early Childhood Students, Exceptional Learners, and Parents

What: A student-centered platform that connects learners with teachers and parents.

How: Simplified check-ins, which can be done independently, or with the support of a teacher or parent.

When: Once a day for five minutes to practice Self-Awareness and build relational trust with a caring adult.

SEL Focus: Self-Awareness, Self-Regulation, Voice, Agency, Positive Youth Identity, Human Connection, and Relational Trust

SEL On Demand: Curated Catalog of SEL Videos

What: An online catalog of SEL videos broken down by grade band (from EC to HS) and duration that can be viewed together as a class or shared as links.

How: Teachers access the video library to find engaging SEL videos varying in length and current topics, such as managing anxiety or anger.

SEL Focus: Self-Awareness, Self-Regulation, Social Awareness, Balance between Social Harmony and Self-Efficacy.

To schedule a free demo of any of the EdTech SEL solutions, please email Rob at hello@classcatalyst.com.

Or, as you dive into the book, please don't hesitate to contact the authors with questions or inquire about their online (live or recorded) and in-person professional learning, coaching, and workshop opportunities. They absolutely love hearing from educators, administrators and parents. Email them directly at carla.p@mindfulpractices.us or allison.slade@mindfulpractices.us.

Acknowledgments

This book was created out of love and the hope of exploring an opportunity for a better tomorrow, a more just world, and a new and enduring acceptance of the importance of relationships, Self-Awareness, and student and adult well-being as the foundation of a healthy classroom and school community.

Allison and Carla would like to thank their collective families for their support along this journey and the patience it necessitates. Mike and Rob—understanding husbands and supportive spouses and Elise, Gaby, Dottie Nola, and Remi—our kids who are less patient, but make it all up in love all deserve our appreciation and thanks. We hope that you and the amazing educators with whom you work can find some positivity and new ways to meet the needs of students as schools continue to evolve.

To our moms—Char and Violet, who taught us to both to be and raise strong women, we are forever grateful. And to our dads—Barry and Pat, who taught us to never give up on our dreams, even when they sounded crazy.

To the entire Mindful Practices team who works tirelessly on a daily basis to make schools and classrooms more whole and supportive places, we are eternally grateful.

Thank you!

Preface

We have all experienced the shift to learning in a virtual environment in different, and sometimes similar ways. In March, 2020, when schools across the country were closed, the period of emergency remote learning began. Chaos in the field of education ensued. Debates around the best way to educate students became furious. A tirade of questions was posed in a matter of moments and debated regularly within schools and communities and in the media and online:

- Should we have more screen time or less screen time?
- What is the difference between synchronous and asynchronous teaching and learning?
- What if you are an essential worker (or a teacher yourself) and you do not have a physically safe place for your own child to learn?
- How do we accurately assess student academic progress? What if your students do/don't make academic progress?
- How do we build relational trust with students?
- How can we assess and address students' SEL, mental health, and well-being needs virtually?
- How can we address the well-being, mental health, and SEL needs of all adult stakeholders who are serving our students?
- How can we infuse culturally responsive, trauma-informed, and anti-racist practices into the fabric of our SEL work?

Fear and uncertainty constantly troubled the minds of adults and children alike. A scholastic earthquake followed and in a matter of moments, schools as we had known them for hundreds of years were being transformed before our eyes. Teachers were heralded as heroes for relentlessly attempting to ensure that learning continued in virtual classrooms across the globe. The focus was on retaining learning through the spring and new learning was put on hold in most places, in favor of maintaining student and staff well-being, and providing a space for teachers to experiment in their new setting. Summer provided a welcome change for all involved, with the perpetual hope that schools would begin again in their comfortable, typical fashion in the fall. Crisis teaching was expected to be over.

However, the fall came, and schools had very little direction on how to prepare while simultaneously dealing with the continuing uncertainty in the world around them. Seventy-one out of the largest 120 school districts nation-wide remained open for virtual learning only. Less than 40 percent of school age children nation-wide began the 2020–2021 school year with in-person learning as an option—that's more than 5.26 million students (Lips, 2020). However, now, the expectations are different. Educators and school leaders are now steeped deeply in the unwelcome knowledge that this was not the fleeting moment of emergency we all expected back in the spring. We would be in this for the "long haul"—a quarter, a semester, a year—or more, until significant advances in science were made. Despite an approved vaccine for adults, the uncertainty of "return to school" still looks to be for an unknown duration, and, if we've learned anything from the last 18 months, we must be prepared to pivot at a moment's notice, always responding in "real time" to student need. The expectations on schools and teachers have increased dramatically as the amount of time for preparation, and the need to become more purposeful and intentional in the virtual environment, became an assumption.

Are We Listening to Our Students?

However, while adults scrambled to create some sense of "normalcy" in the opening of the school year, we often neglected the voices of the very children who were experiencing the upheaval. As Carla states in her book, *Everyday SEL*, "If SEL is going to be both relevant and sensitive to the needs of today's youth, adults need to stop guessing what children are thinking and feeling and pause to take the time to ask them. Then, listen." While preparing this text, we decided to take our own advice, and ask some children who have been experiencing virtual learning, and virtual SEL, for more than ten months to describe their thoughts and feelings around the changing realities of the new school year.

Defining Remote/Virtual Instruction for the Future

While it is widely recognized that the emergency remote learning period that defined the period from March 2020 through the end of the 2019–2020 school year is complete, we have entered a new "normal" in which teaching and learning will encompass multiple modalities in ways we have yet to imagine in the field of education. Our working definition of remote or virtual instruction is not the same as "online" learning. Our working assumption is that, while various models and modalities will be utilized with remote or virtual instruction, these terms encompass a teacher role that occurs both synchronously and asynchronously, rather than online teaching which is widely defined as self-paced and encompasses a distinct design process. Researchers in educational technology have carefully defined terms over the years to distinguish between the highly variable design solutions that have been developed and implemented but are clear that these do NOT qualify as emergency remote teaching: distance learning, distributed learning, blended learning, online learning, mobile learning, and others. As teachers and leaders ourselves, we see this new remote/virtual teaching world as relevant long beyond the COVID-19 crisis—where the opportunities for its use are abundant for students with significant and ongoing medical needs, for migrant students, and even for severe weather or snow days, just to name a few. Therefore, in our view, these strategies and opportunities that lie in the creation of this text for SEL in a virtual classroom can be useful in the long-term, and possibly in ways we have yet to devise as our "new normal" takes shape.

Below is a transcribed interview we conducted of Alana (age 13) and Caroline (age 10) on social emotional learning, cool down strategies, and why managing feelings can sometimes be hard, especially in the virtual environment. As you implement SEL and mindfulness in your classroom, and perhaps at home, we encourage you to take a moment to ask the youth you serve what they think and feel about the skills you are asking them to practice. What works? What doesn't? Why? Not only will this inform your work as a practitioner, but it will also demonstrate to your students (and children at home) that their voices matter and by using their words they can positively influence how the world around them operates.

Me: *What is Social Emotional Learning?*

Alana: We have a class called social emotional learning. We learn behavior skills, empathy and . . . we used to have it once a week [in-person], but now we have it once a day [remote learning]. We learn about helping others and helping ourselves on Mondays and then the teachers meet individually with us other days of the week. I personally like it, I know other kids do not because we learn the same thing every single year and they think it is babyish.

Caroline: I don't like that we have homework to do and we have to do it with an adult and they have to sign it. It isn't real.

Me: *Why is SEL important in school?*

Alana: I think it is important to learn in school because they are life skills I guess. For example, if you don't know how to give empathy people are not going to like you. And like helping yourself—if you don't do self-care you can't help others.

But not everyone thinks it is important. You can tell when the teachers don't like it. The kids will tell you they don't do the lessons, or they rush through the lessons so they can take a "week off" or whatever. I haven't had a teacher do this, but other kids talk about it.

Me: *How is it different in a virtual setting?*

Alana: I mean, everything is different now. You have to practice different types of self-care now. So instead of teaching like in the class we learn about things that happen in school but now we talk about online things. Like being kind online, like in social media.

Now it is more about getting through the pandemic and how you can get through looking at a screen all day more than helping others. They realize that we are on our devices much more so we are on social media more and cyberbullying is a lot more of an issue. We talk about how to be helping yourself online and not in-person now.

We have synchronous and asynchronous time now at our school. Our classes are 80 minutes so we are on screen for 60 minutes and then at the end we ask questions. We aren't used to that because our blocks in school are 40 minutes. They gave us different strategies for doing asynchronous work like going outside for a walk after ten minutes of work. Do whatever makes you happy. When I meet with my teacher once a week we talk about what makes me happy and what I can do to help myself when I am feeling stressed. The teacher gives me an extra push on how to take care of ourselves.

Me: *Tell me more about that.*

Alana: It is a totally different surrounding. What they taught us in normal school they had to because it was a different environment but some of the things we are learning now are things we should learn about in school. Like bullying online. In school self-care is different than online self-care. So there are definitely things that we are learning in SEL now that we should have learned in school. . . . I hope they continue these lessons.

Me: *What do you do when your feelings or emotions feel out of control?*

Alana: Honestly, I do one of two things. I always feel better when I go outside. I put in headphones and listen to my favorite music and walk outside without a specific place to go, just wander around. A second thing I do is to look up my emotion on YouTube and play music and dance and improvise in my living room.

And, I get to do these things now because we are at home. One thing I like about the virtual setting is I get to pick and structure my lunch period more than in school. That is our break and when we practice our self-care. I like that more during remote learning than in school because I have more control.

Directory of Terms

1. *Agency*: Student agency refers to learning through activities that are meaningful and relevant to learners, driven by their interests, and often self-initiated with appropriate guidance from teachers. To put it simply, student agency gives students voice and often, choice, in how they learn. Their ability to make a decision triggers a greater investment of interest and motivation.
   SOURCE: "Student Agency." *Renaissance EdWords*. www.renaissance. com/edwords/student-agency/. Accessed March 2, 2021.

2. *Anti-racism*: The active process of identifying and eliminating racism by changing systems, organizational structures, policies and practices, and attitudes so that power is redistributed and shared equitably.
   SOURCE: *The National Action Committee on the Status of Women International Perspectives: Women and Global Solidarity*. University of Massachusetts Amherst, Office of the Provost website, 2021. www.umass.edu/provost/resources/all-resources/faculty-diversity/ anti-racism-resources. Accessed March 29, 2021.

3. *Anti-racist Pedagogy*: A paradigm located within Critical Theory utilized to explain and counteract the persistence and impact of racism praxis as its focus to promote social justice for the creation of a democratic society in every respect.
   SOURCE: Blakeney, A.M. (2011). Antiracist pedagogy: Definition, theory, purpose, and professional development. *Journal of Curriculum & Pedagogy* 2(1), 119–132.

4. *Asynchronous Learning*: Asynchronous learning is a student-centered teaching method widely used in online learning. Its basic premise is that learning can occur in different times and spaces particular to each learner, as opposed to synchronous learning at the same time and place with groups of learners and their instructor, or one learner and their instructor. In asynchronous learning, instructors usually set up a learning path, which students engage with at their own pace.
   SOURCE: Finol, M. O. (2020). "Asynchronous vs. Synchronous Learning: A Quick Overview." From Bryn Mawr College "Blended Learning" website. Posted March 26, 2020. www.brynmawr.edu/

blendedlearning/asynchronous-vs-synchronous-learning-quick-overview. Accessed March 29, 2021.

5. ***Authentic Student Voice***: The student voice is the thoughts, views, and opinions of students on an educational journey. Engaging all students, not just those who volunteer regularly, to use their voices to incorporate their knowledge, life experiences, and cultures allows students to authentically lead, make decisions, and solve problems. Authentic student voice is an asset for all school communities.
SOURCE: CASEL Guide to Schoolwide SEL, 2021. https://schoolguide. casel.org/focus-area-3/school/elevate-student-voice/. Accessed June 29, 2021.

6. ***Breath Work***: Conscious, controlled breathing done especially for relaxation, meditation, or therapeutic purposes.
SOURCE: Merriam-Webster. (n.d.). Breath work. In *Merriam-Webster. com dictionary*. www.merriam-webster.com/dictionary/breath%20 work. Accessed February 25, 2021.

7. ***Compassion***: Sympathetic <u>consciousness</u> of others' distress together with a desire to alleviate it. Self-compassion refers to the ability to turn understanding, love, and acceptance inward toward oneself.
SOURCES: "Compassion." *Merriam-Webster.com Dictionary*, Merriam-Webster, www.merriam-webster.com/dictionary/compassion. Accessed March 2, 2021. "Self-Compassion." *GoodTherapy.org*, GoodTherapy, www.goodtherapy.org/learn-about-therapy/issues/ self-compassion. Accessed March 2, 2021.

8. ***Consciousness***: Consciousness refers to your individual awareness of your unique thoughts, memories, feelings, sensations, and environments. Essentially, your consciousness is your awareness of yourself and the world around you. This awareness is subjective and unique to you, and is constantly shifting and changing. If you can describe something you are experiencing in words, then it is part of your consciousness.
SOURCE: Cherry, K. (2020). Theories: Cognitive Psychology: What Is Consciousness? Very Well Mind. www.verywellmind.com/ what-is-consciousness-2795922. Accessed March 29, 2021.

9. ***Culturally Responsive Teaching***: A pedagogy that recognizes the importance of including students' cultural references in all aspects of learning. Culturally responsive teaching acknowledges, responds to, and celebrates fundamental cultures and offers full, equitable access

to education for students from all cultures. Some of the characteristics of culturally responsive teaching are:

1. Positive perspectives on parents and families
2. Communication of high expectations
3. Learning within the context of culture
4. Student-centered instruction
5. Culturally mediated instruction
6. Reshaping the curriculum
7. Teacher as facilitator

SOURCE: Ladson-Billings, G. (1994). *The Dreamkeepers*. San Francisco: Jossey-Bass Publishing Co.

10. ***Digital and/or Remote Learning***: Digital, or remote learning provides an opportunity for students and teachers to remain connected and engaged with the content while working from their homes. Opportunities for remote learning are typically linked to emergency situations that pose a threat to student safety. It is important to note that in remote learning environments, versus virtual learning environments, the learner and teacher are not accustomed to having distance during instruction. This may pose a challenge to both teacher and learner that can be accommodated through specific support structures. Remote learning is different from virtual school or virtual learning programs that typically have gone through an official process of establishing a school, adopting an online curriculum, and creating a dedicated structure to support students enrolled in the school. eLearning utilizes electronic technologies to access educational curriculum outside of the traditional classroom.

SOURCE: Ray, K. (2020). *Remote Learning Playbook*. www.techlearning.com/news/remote-learning-playbook-free-special-report-from-tech-and-learning. Accessed August 23, 2021.

11. ***Dysregulation***: Dysregulation, also known as emotional dysregulation, refers to a poor ability to manage emotional responses or to keep them within an acceptable range of typical emotional reactions. This can refer to a wide range of emotions including sadness, anger, irritability, and frustration. While emotional dysregulation is typically thought of as a childhood problem that usually resolves itself as a child learns proper emotional regulation skills and strategies, emotional dysregulation may continue into adulthood.

SOURCE: Cuncic, A. (2021). Emotions: What Is Dysregulation? Very Well Mind. www.verywellmind.com/what-is-dysregulation-5073868. Accessed March 29, 2021.

12. *EdTech*: A term combining "education" and "technology" that refers to hardware and software designed to enhance teacher-led learning in classrooms and improve students' education outcomes.
SOURCE: Frankenfield, J. (2020). EdTech. Investopedia. www.investopedia.com/terms/e/edtech.asp. Accessed March 29, 2021.

13. *Educators*: A collective term for employees working within a school or district who have direct interaction with students, including teachers, paraprofessionals, aides, coaches, instructors, specialists, etc.
SOURCE: Mindful Practices. (2021).

14. *Human Connection*: An energy exchange between people who are paying attention to one another. It has the power to deepen the moment, inspire change, and build trust. At Mindful Practices, this often involves play, communication, and collaboration.
SOURCE: Pisacano Brown, D. (2018). "The power of human connection." LI Herald. www.liherald.com/stories/the-power-of-human-connection,102632. Accessed March 29, 2021.

15. *Hybrid Schedule*: A way of combining traditional in-person classroom experiences, experiential learning objectives, and digital (online) course delivery that emphasizes using the best option for each learning objective.
SOURCE: "What is Hybrid Learning? How to Implement a Hybrid Learning Strategy." From eThink blog and website. Posted Nov. 20, 2020. https://ethinkeducation.com/blog/what-is-hybrid-learning-how-to-implement-a-hybrid-learning-strategy/. Accessed March 29, 2021.

16. *Instructional Time*: The amount of time during which learners receive instruction from a classroom teacher in a school or a virtual context. Intended instructional time is usually specified in school or education policies or regulations.
SOURCE: International Bureau of Education, UNESCO. (2013).

17. *Intentionality*: Deliberate action moving past tendencies. The opposite of "responding on autopilot" or falling back into the same narrative. This requires disciplined habits of mind ownership.
SOURCE: Mindful Practices. (2021).

18. *Interpersonal*: Being, relating to, or involving relations between persons.
SOURCE: "Interpersonal." *Merriam-Webster.com Dictionary*, Merriam-Webster, www.merriam-webster.com/dictionary/interpersonal. Accessed March 2, 2021.

19. *Intrapersonal*: Occurring within the individual mind or self.
   SOURCE: "Intrapersonal." *Merriam-Webster.com Dictionary*, Merriam-Webster, www.merriam-webster.com/dictionary/intrapersonal. Accessed March 2, 2021.

20. *LGBTQIA2S+*: An acronym for Lesbian, Gay, Bisexual, Transgender, Queer and/or Questioning, Intersex, Asexual, Two-Spirit, and the countless affirmative ways in which people choose to self-identify.
   SOURCE: Portland Art Museum. https://portlandartmuseum.org/learn/programs-tours/object-stories/powerful-self-lgbtqia2s-lives-today/. Accessed March 29, 2021.

21. *Meditation*: To engage in contemplation or reflection; to engage in mental exercise (such as concentration on one's breathing or repetition of a mantra) for the purpose of reaching a heightened level of spiritual awareness.
   SOURCE: "Meditate." *Merriam-Webster.com Dictionary*, Merriam-Webster, www.merriam-webster.com/dictionary/meditate. Accessed February 25, 2021.

22. *Mindfulness*: The awareness that emerges through paying attention on purpose, Jon Kabat-Zinn. Mindfulness means maintaining a moment-by-moment awareness of our thoughts, feelings, bodily sensations, and surrounding environment, through a gentle, nurturing lens. Mindfulness also involves acceptance, meaning that we pay attention to our thoughts and feelings without judging them—without believing, for instance, that there's a "right" or "wrong" way to think or feel in a given moment. When we practice mindfulness, our thoughts tune into what we're sensing in the present moment rather than rehashing the past or imagining the future.
   SOURCE: "Mindfulness Defined: What is Mindfulness?" *Greater Good Magazine*, 2021. https://greatergood.berkeley.edu/topic/mindfulness/definition. Accessed March 29, 2021.

23. *Mindful Practices:* Mindfulness is one of the vehicles or Mindful Practices we use to create space for stillness. Mindful practices require space to first cultivate the bedrock intrapersonal competency of Self-Awareness, which leads to SEL growth in other competency areas. This book examines the interplay between interpersonal and intrapersonal SEL skill development and how the practices of vocalization, movement, stillness, and teamwork, or what we call *Mindful Practices* develop not only one's Self-Awareness but, in turn, an

increased ability for one to form positive human connections with others.

SOURCE: Mindful Practices. (2021).

24. *Movement*: Physical motion between points in space. It is the combination of the physicality of skill development combined with the artistry of self-expression. Conceptually, movement is organized as Space, Time, Force, and Body. At Mindful Practices, we consider movement to involve yoga, dance, fitness, and stretching.

SOURCE: Green Gilbert, A. (1992). *Creative Dance for All Ages*, 2nd Edition.

25. *Native and Indigenous Peoples*: Also referred to as First peoples, Aboriginal peoples, or autochthonous peoples, are ethnic groups who are native to a particular place on Earth and live or lived in an interconnected relationship with the natural environment there for many generations prior to the arrival of non-Indigenous peoples.

SOURCE: Indigenous Peoples. (2021, February 25). In Wikipedia. https://en.wikipedia.org/wiki/Indigenous_peoples. Accessed March 29, 2021.

26. *Non-Instructional Time*: Time set aside by the school before actual classroom instruction begins or after actual classroom instruction ends.

SOURCE: 20 USCS § 4072 (4) [Title 20. Education; Chapter 52. Education for Economic Security; Equal Access https://definitions.uslegal.com/n/noninstructional-time-education/. Accessed March 29, 2021.

27. *Non-Judgmentalness*: Noticing yourself (thoughts, words, deeds) and the world around you without evaluation, appraisal, assessment or the need to label (actions, feelings or emotions) *good* or *bad*. Clarity.

SOURCE: Mindful Practices. (2021).

28. *People of Color (POC)*: Often the preferred collective term for referring to non-white racial groups. Racial justice advocates have been using the term "people of color" (not to be confused with the pejorative "colored people") since the late 1970s as an inclusive and unifying frame across different racial groups that are not white, to address racial inequities. While "people of color" can be a politically useful term, and describes people with their own attributes (as opposed to what they are not, e.g., "non-white"), it is also important whenever possible to identify people through their own racial/ethnic group, as each has its own distinct experience and meaning and may be more appropriate. Some people choose to capitalize "People of Color,"

while others choose not to; while there is not a "correct" capitalization rule, it is most often a term that is seen capitalized.

SOURCE: (2015). Race Forward, *Race Reporting Guide*. The Center for Racial Justice Innovation. www.raceforward.org/reporting-guide. Accessed March 29, 2021.

29. ***Positive Youth Identity***: Identity refers to how one defines themselves in terms of values, beliefs, and their role in the world. Self-identity in adolescence forms the basis of our self-esteem later in life. Youth identity is the result of various internal and external factors. The development of clear and positive identity/identities involves building self-esteem, facilitating exploration of and commitment to self-definition, reducing self-discrepancies, and fostering role formation and achievement.

SOURCE: Watson, J., Aspiro Adventure, and Tsang, S. K. M., Hui, E. K. P., & Law, B. C. M. Positive identity as a positive youth development construct: A conceptual review. *The Scientific World Journal*, Article ID 529691, 8 pages. https://doi.org/10.1100/2012/529691

30. ***Practices***: To perform (an activity) or work at (a skill) repeatedly so as to become proficient. At Mindful Practices, we consider these practices to be in connection with Self-Awareness, movement, mindfulness, regulation, etc.

SOURCE: "Practice." *Merriam-Webster.com Dictionary*, Merriam-Webster, www.merriam-webster.com/dictionary/practice. Accessed February 25, 2021.

31. ***School Connectedness***: School connectedness is the belief held by students that adults and peers in the school care about their learning as well as about them as individuals. Students are more likely to engage in healthy behaviors and succeed academically when they feel connected to school. School connectedness is particularly important for young people who are at increased risk for feeling alienated or isolated from others. Those at greater risk for feeling disconnected include students with disabilities, LGBTQIA2S+ students, students who are homeless, or any student who is chronically truant due to a variety of circumstances. Strong family involvement and supportive school personnel, inclusive school environments, and curricula that reflect the realities of a diverse student body can help students become more connected to their school.

SOURCE: "School Connectedness." American Psychological Association. (2014). www.apa.orSaxg/pi/lgbt/programs/safe-supportive/school-connectedness. Accessed March 29, 2021.

32. **School Stakeholders**: Typically refers to anyone who is invested in the welfare and success of a school and its students, including administrators, teachers, staff members, students, parents, families, community members, local business leaders, and elected officials such as school board members, city councilors, and state representatives. Stakeholders have a "stake" in the school and its students, meaning that they have personal, professional, civic, or financial interest or concern.
    SOURCE: "Stakeholder." The Glossary of Education Reform. (2014). www.edglossary.org/stakeholder/. Accessed March 29, 2021.

33. **Self-Awareness**: The abilities to understand one's own emotions, thoughts, feelings, and values and how they influence behavior across contexts, including impact on your physical self. This includes capacities to recognize one's strengths and limitations with a well-grounded sense of confidence and purpose, as well as the ability to take ownership for the emotions you have and understanding your power of choice in response to those emotions.
    SOURCE: "SEL: What Are the Core Competence Areas and Where are they Promoted?" CASEL website. (2020). https://casel.org/sel-framework/. Accessed June 29, 2021.

34. **Self-Management**: The ability to manage one's emotions, thoughts, and behaviors effectively in different situations and to achieve goals and aspirations. This includes the capacity to delay gratification, manage stress, and feel motivation and agency to accomplish personal/collective goals.
    SOURCE: "SEL: What Are the Core Competence Areas and Where are they Promoted?" CASEL website. (2020). https://casel.org/sel-framework/. Accessed June 29, 2021.

35. **Simultaneous Teaching**: Students, whether choosing or able to attend school remotely or in-person, are learning the same content, together, but some are not physically present while others are.
    SOURCE: Fister, D. G. & Frey, N. (2020). "Simultaneous Learning: Blending Physical and Remote Learning." From Teaching Channel blog and website. Posted Oct. 6, 2020. www.teachingchannel.com/blog/simultaneous-learning. Accessed March 29, 2021.

36. **Singularity**: The ability to focus on a single task at hand; the opposite of multitasking. Being fully present and engaged with one thing at a time. Space to learn and hear what our bodies are telling us. Awareness.
    SOURCE: Mindful Practices. (2021).

37. **Social Awareness**: The ability to understand the perspectives of and empathize with others, including those from diverse backgrounds, cultures and contexts. This includes the capacity to feel compassion for others, understand broader historical and social norms for behavior in different settings, and recognize family, school, and community resources and supports.
SOURCE: "SEL: What Are the Core Competence Areas and Where are they Promoted?" CASEL website. (2020). https://casel.org/sel-framework/. Accessed June 29, 2021.

38. **Social Emotional Competence (SEC)**: The ability to interact with others, regulate one's own emotions and behavior, solve problems, and communicate effectively.

   ◆ **Self-Awareness**: Building this competency cultivates an awareness of self, empowering the learner with the self-knowledge to better address their mental, emotional, and well-being needs.
   ◆ **Self-Regulation**: Building this competency constructs the bridge from awareness to regulation and can shift the learner from impulsivity to intentional navigation of behavioral choices.
   ◆ **Social Awareness**: Building this competency cultivates an awareness of self in social situations; what we bring into the room and how the energy and atmosphere in the room impacts us. By building this competency the learner can move from a reactive mindset to a more proactive, communal view of their role in the world around them.
   ◆ **Self-Efficacy and Social Harmony**: When in balance, the learner feels centered, present, and like a valued and contributing member of the world around them. This competency also reflects the learner's ability to find their voice and to use actionable insights to balance the needs of the self with the needs of others without excessive self-sacrifice.

   SOURCE: "Social-Emotional Competence of Children: Protective and Promotive Factors." Center for the Study of Social Policy. (2018). https://cssp.org/wp-content/uploads/2018/08/HO-2.1e-CW-Social-Emotional-Competence.pdf. Accessed March 29, 2021.

39. **Social Emotional Learning (SEL)**: The process through which all young people and adults acquire and apply the knowledge, skills, and attitudes to develop healthy identities, manage emotions, and achieve personal and collective goals, feel and show empathy for others, establish and maintain supportive relationships, and make responsible

and caring decisions. SEL advances educational equity and excellence through authentic school–family–community partnerships to establish learning environments and experiences that feature trusting and collaborative relationships, rigorous and meaningful curriculum and instruction, and ongoing evaluation. SEL can help address various forms of inequity and empower young people and adults to co-create thriving schools and contribute to safe, healthy, and just communities. SOURCE: "SEL is . . . " CASEL website. (2020). https://casel.org/what-is-sel/. Accessed June 29, 2021.

40. ***Social (or Socio) Emotional Well-Being***: Healthy social, emotional, and behavioral well-being is defined as a child's developing capacity to:

   ◆ Form close, secure, meaningful relationships
   ◆ Experience, regulate, and express emotions
   ◆ Explore the environment and learn new skills

   SOURCE: "Social Emotional Well-Being." The Kaleidoscope Project. (2019). www.kaleidoscopewake.org/social-emotional-well-being. Accessed March 29, 2021.

41. ***(Creating) Space***: Creating mental, emotional, and physical marginality in your life. The space to respond compassionately to different personal and social triggers without losing one's center or sacrificing social rapport. The opposite of dysfunctional *groupthink* or habitual, unconscious reactions to everyday events. Consciousness. SOURCE: Mindful Practices. (2021).

42. ***Stillness***: A state of freedom from storm or disturbance; quietness; silence; calmness. Mindful Practices often refers to stillness reached through meditation, reflection, breath work, and/or mindfulness. Stillness of the body does not necessarily mean the mind is still—our thoughts still persist. However, continued stillness of the body can lead to stillness of the mind. SOURCE: "Stillness." *Merriam-Webster.com Thesaurus*, Merriam-Webster, www.merriam-webster.com/thesaurus/stillness. Accessed February 25, 2021.

43. ***Students (Young People) Who Have Experienced Trauma***: A traumatic event is a frightening, dangerous, or violent event that poses a threat to a child's life or bodily integrity. Witnessing a traumatic event that threatens the life or physical security of a loved one can also be traumatic. This is particularly important for young children as their sense of safety depends on the perceived safety of their attachment figures. Traumatic experiences can initiate strong

emotions and physical reactions that can persist long after the event. Traumatic events can occur outside of the family (such as a natural disaster, car accident, school shooting, or community violence) or from within the family, such as domestic violence, physical or sexual abuse, or the unexpected death of a loved one.

SOURCE: "About Childhood Trauma." American Academy of Pediatrics. The National Child Traumatic Stress Network. www.nctsn.org/what-is-child-trauma/about-child-trauma. Accessed March 29, 2021.

44. *Synchronous Learning*: Synchronous learning refers to all types of learning in which learner(s) and instructor(s) are in the same place, at the same time, in order for learning to take place, and generally includes in-person classes. In synchronous learning, students usually go through the learning path together, accompanied by their instructor who is able to provide support while students are completing tasks and activities.

SOURCE: Finol, M. O. (2020). "Asynchronous vs. Synchronous Learning: A Quick Overview." From Bryn Mawr College "Blended Learning" website. Posted March 26, 2020. www.brynmawr.edu/blendedlearning/asynchronous-vs-synchronous-learning-quick-overview. Accessed March 29, 2021.

45. *Trauma-Informed Practices*: A trauma-informed practice is defined as an organizational structure and treatment framework that involves understanding, recognizing, and responding to the effects of all types of trauma.

SOURCE: "Becoming a Trauma-Informed Practice." American Academy of Pediatrics. www.aap.org/en-us/advocacy-and-policy/aap-health-initiatives/resilience/Pages/Becoming-a-Trauma-Informed-Practice.aspx. Accessed March 29, 2021.

46. *Trauma-Informed Systems*: A trauma-informed child and family service system is one in which all parties involved recognize and respond to the impact of traumatic stress on those who have contact with the system including children, caregivers, and service providers.

SOURCE: The National Child Traumatic Stress Network.

47. *Vocalization*: To express oneself or use the voice to articulate a need, issue, or thought. Can be through speaking, chanting, singing, or other forms of sound.

SOURCE: "Vocalize." *Merriam-Webster.com Dictionary*, Merriam-Webster, www.merriam-webster.com/dictionary/vocalize. Accessed February 25, 2021.

48. *Voice*: In education, student voice refers to the values, opinions, beliefs, perspectives, and cultural backgrounds of individual students and groups of students in a school, and to instructional approaches and techniques that are based on student choices, interests, passions, and ambitions.
SOURCE: "Student Voice." *The Glossary for Education Reform*, updated December 12, 2013. www.edglossary.org/student-voice/. Accessed March 29, 2021.

49. *Vulnerable Learners*: A student or someone who has no access or limited access to basic needs such as sufficient and nutritious food, shelter, adequate clothing, a safe home and community environment free from abuse and exploitation, family care and support, good healthcare, and the ability to take full advantage of available education opportunities.
SOURCE: Bialobrezeska, M., Randell, C., Hellmann, L., Winkler, G. (2009). "Creating a Caring School: A Guide and Toolkit for School Management Teams." South African Institute for Distance Education (SAIDE). www.saide.org.za/documents/Toolkit.pdf. Accessed March 29, 2021.

50. *Well-Being*: is the experience of health, <u>happiness</u>, and prosperity. It includes having good mental health, high life satisfaction, a sense of meaning or purpose, and <u>ability to manage stress</u>. More generally, well-being is just feeling well; happy, healthy, socially connected, and purposeful.
SOURCE: Davis, T. (2019). "What Is Well-Being? Definition, Types, and Well-Being Skills." Psychology Today. www.psychologytoday.com/us/blog/click-here-happiness/201901/what-is-well-being-definition-types-and-well-being-skills. Accessed March 29, 2021.

51. *Yoga*: A system of physical postures, breathing techniques, and sometimes meditation derived from Yoga (Hindu theistic philosophy) but often practiced independently especially in Western cultures to promote physical and emotional well-being.
SOURCE: "Yoga." *Merriam-Webster.com Dictionary*, Merriam-Webster, www.merriam-webster.com/dictionary/yoga. Accessed February 25, 2021.

Introduction

So, What *Is* Social Emotional Learning?

CASEL defines Social Emotional Learning as: *the process through which all young people and adults acquire and apply the knowledge, skills, and attitudes to develop healthy identities, manage emotions and achieve personal and collective goals, feel and show empathy for others, establish and maintain supportive relationships, and make responsible and caring decisions.*

SEL advances educational equity and excellence through authentic school–family–community partnerships to establish learning environments and experiences that feature trusting and collaborative relationships, rigorous and meaningful curriculum and instruction, and ongoing evaluation. SEL can help address various forms of inequity and empower young people and adults to co-create thriving schools and contribute to safe, healthy, and just communities.

While this definition is very useful, it can feel cumbersome if we are new to the discipline. When working with educators across the country, I will ask folks what SEL means to them. As boots on the ground caring adults who teach or work with youth every day, they responded:

SEL is a way to slow and calm the mind in order to be aware of our emotions and to be aware of what really matters so students (and adults!) can be happier, healthier people!

SEL is learning about self and your relationships with others. Students can learn this by: connecting authentically with adults, by getting to know themselves and when I fuse SEL into academic content.

DOI: 10.4324/9781003183204-1

SEL is an ongoing process, a journey without end just as self-improvement is never ending. It's continuous building on previous growth. It's improving upon each improvement.

As an educator, I use SEL in two ways: to build an interpersonal connection with my students before class starts (non-instructional time) AND to build my students' awareness of their own emotions to prevent frustration, stress and/or performance anxiety from negatively impacting their achievement.

SEL is the lifelong process of understanding your emotions and how to manage them.

To me, SEL is an ongoing, reciprocal process between students, peers, adults, staff, where everyone learns how to respond (rather than react) to stressful or disturbing situations, creating an atmosphere of safety and empathy.

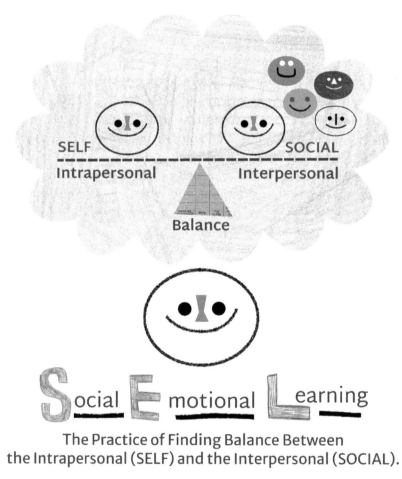

Figure 0.1 SEL The Balance between Intrapersonal and Interpersonal

Social Emotional Learning during a global pandemic has taken on new importance to schools, teachers, and families, specifically with the loss of connection we have all experienced after living the better part of a year without a physical connection with others outside of our immediate families. As Brené Brown reminds us in her work, *Daring Greatly* (2012) "Connection is why we're here. We are hardwired to connect with others, it's what gives purpose and meaning to our lives, and without it there is suffering" (p. 145). And, without this invaluable connection, we have seen many students (and adults) flounder.

The research is clear: SEL is key to successful student performance, especially in preschool and elementary school (Vega, 2012). It is also clear that students, teachers, and school leaders alike are struggling to reimagine what school, and its socio-emotional support, should look like for students when they are in school remotely, in-person in a new way, or a hybrid of the two. And, it is clear that the impact of this time period on student's overall mental health, future earnings and performance, could be greater than we even know now. Beyond the need for teachers and school leaders to continue to connect with students, the challenge becomes one of sustaining themselves when also dealing with the secondary trauma (Walker, 2019) associated with students and families who are dealing with the acute, repeated trauma that comes with an ongoing pandemic.

This book will help teachers, school and district leaders, and parents with implementing specific strategies in an environment where disconnection is prevalent due to the virtual or remote nature of school—both during a pandemic and beyond. This book starts and ends with the adult community, as building school connectedness, youth agency, and social responsibility begins with Self-Awareness and reflection and recognition of how the current virtual environment is impacting YOU.

SEL Implementation and Integration

Becoming an emotionally intelligent educator in the face of uncertainty is fundamental to creating and sustaining emotionally healthy classroom and school environments. Hattie (2018) articulated the crucial nature of these student and adult skills in his series of meta-analyses in *Visible Learning* with the following conclusions.

- ◆ Fostering student Self-Regulation is crucial for moving learning to deep and transfer levels. (Self-Awareness, Self-Regulation).
- ◆ Feedback in a high trust environment must be integrated into the learning cycle. (School Connectedness).
- ◆ Well-designed peer-learning impacts understanding. (Social Awareness, Agency).
- ◆ Learning accelerates when the student, not the teacher, is taught to be in control of learning. (Voice, Agency, Positive Youth Identity).

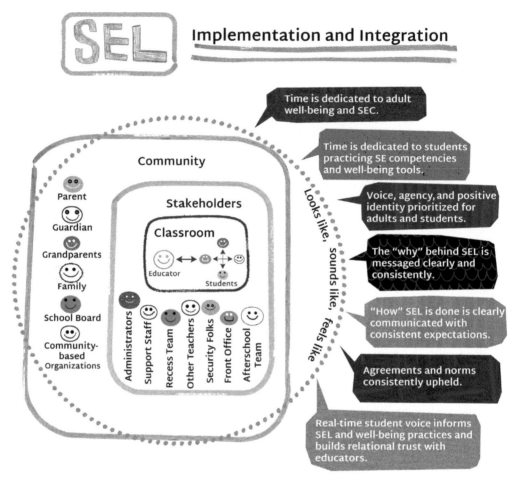

Figure 0.2 SEL Implementation and Integration

Fisher, Frey, and Hattie (2020) state, "These themes transcend the delivery method. Whether face to face or in virtual or distance environments, these themes endure" (p. 3). Therefore, we, the authors, have decided to connect the upcoming chapters and activities with these research based conclusions that positively impact student achievement at all developmental levels of instruction. We have linked Hattie's research to our own Mindful Practices model, and clearly articulated the connections between our recommended activities and ongoing practices with the evidence about what works to best impact student success. Each chapter has been carefully designed to include examples and activities across the K-12 spectrum not only to apply to many educators, but also to reinforce the developmental continuum that exists as students go through the grade levels and the connections we can make across a school setting to continually practice, reinforce, and grow our capacities in each of these SEL domains.

As noted in Table 1.1, in addition to focusing on the social emotional learning activities for students to develop competency, we have added several areas that apply to adults within and outside of the learning environment who interact regularly with students. This adult–student connection piece, whether with teachers who are collaboratively planning and engaging in growing their social emotional competence in professional development

Table 1.1 This table aligns the Mindful Practices exercises and activities with SEL competencies for adults and children to be developed in a virtual setting

Chapter	Research Base	Activities Included
Chapter 1: *Becoming Emotionally Intelligent in a Virtual Teaching Environment*	Teachers and leaders with a high socio-emotional competence are better prepared to engage their students in social emotional learning.	• Developing Norms • Cultivating Relaxed Alertness • Mindful Practices Model
Chapter 2: *Creating the Climate and Conditions for a Socio-Emotionally Healthy Virtual Classroom*	The classroom, or learning space, is often referred to as the third teacher—critical for facilitating learning success.	• Thumb Check • POP Check • Digital Agreements • Talking Stick
Chapter 3: *Self-Awareness and Self-Regulation*	Fostering student Self-Regulation is crucial for moving learning to deep and transfer levels.	• Draw and Rip • Write and Rip • Focused Breath • Memory Minute • Equal Breath
Chapter 4: *School Connectedness and Teacher Trust*	Feedback in a high trust environment must be integrated into the learning cycle.	• Tap Our Worries Away • Color Breath • Holding Who I am • Compliment Partners
Chapter 5: *Social Awareness*	Well-designed peer-learning impacts understanding.	• One Word Check-in • Shoulder Share • Gratitude Journal

Chapter	Research Base	Activities Included
Chapter 6: *Student Voice and Agency*	Learning accelerates when the student, not the teacher, is taught to be in control of learning.	• Owning my story • Goal Setting Postcard • Service Learning Project
Chapter 7: *Virtual SEL for Collaborative Planning with Colleagues*	Practicing SEL competencies and skills is critical for ongoing development by adults and students. Integrating these into regular planning sessions is critical for teacher development.	• Spider Web Connecting & Owning My Own Story • Holistic Self-Care Wheel • Compassion Fatigue • Body Scan
Chapter 8: *Engaging Families in SEL in the Virtual Environment*	Engaged families positively impact student performance in school and in life.	• Thumb Check at Home • POP Check at Home

and team settings, or parents connecting with their children through school based opportunities, is important to acknowledge and recognize the critical role all adults play in the development of these skills and competencies in students. We hope our approach throughout this text provides a roadmap for this development in an ever changing virtual setting.

1

Becoming Emotionally Intelligent in a Virtual Teaching Environment

Becoming an emotionally intelligent teacher is a journey and process, with no finality or end point. This is echoed in Theodore Roosevelt's famous quote, "No one cares how much you know, until they know how much you care" (Bishop, 1920). Emotionally intelligent teachers are actively introspective and reflective in their orientation to students, families, the classroom, the school community, and in their own homes and lives. They are resilient in response to negative stress and less likely to overwhelm themselves with pessimism and strong, negative emotions. An ongoing experience in a typical environment, becoming an emotionally intelligent teacher in a virtual teaching environment is even more challenging. This is because this new environment is a new trauma. Perhaps you are a rookie teacher who just got the hang of teaching last fall, and then were upended in the spring. Or, you were moved to teach a new grade level you've never taught before. You could even be a veteran teacher, who has been nimble and part of many different grade levels, but not a regular user of technology. The new requirements and expectations in the virtual setting came on immediately and without warning, and acted much like traumatic experiences but can be mitigated by deliberately working on becoming an emotionally intelligent teacher, even in this virtual setting.

Becoming an emotionally intelligent educator in the virtual setting involves the following steps, some of which occur naturally during in-person

DOI: 10.4324/9781003183204-2

learning, but must be deliberately planned for, and practiced in the virtual setting for all educators.

1. Creating daily routines and working norms: morning, breaks, workplace, after school, among others.
2. Ensuring weekly connections with other adults: professionally and outside the school environment.
3. Creating and promoting a state of relaxed alertness in yourself to promote cognitive engagement in teaching and learning.

We want to be clear that while the aforementioned steps are also critical for students, this section is specifically focused solely on the needs of educators

A Lifelong Practice to Develop Social Emotional Competence (SEC)

Pause.

Breath & Awareness

Own it.

Voice & Connection

Practice.

Choice, Agency & Positive Identity

Figure 1.1 The POP Check

to become emotionally intelligent and develop and practice teaching competencies and corresponding skills for success.

A great first step is to take a sober look at your energetic resources. As Lara Veon discusses in the book, *Everyday Self-Care for Educators* (2019), creating a Self-Care Wheel can be an effective way to assess "both the energy expenditures and replenishers in the holistic areas of well-being (which) allows one to prioritize needs for optimal well-being to live a balanced life." (p. 34). By using the wheel and guiding questions that follow as a guide, you can create a list of energy expenditures and energy replenishers for each category. For example, on the list for physical, you might write about walking the dog or practicing yoga. Also we strongly recommend practicing a POP Check when you feel dysregulated.

Routines and Working Norms: Intrapersonal Emotional Intelligence (SELF)

While working in a school setting, our routines and norms develop naturally out of external expectations. For example, as a teacher I was required to "clock in" by 7:50 am, therefore, working backwards, I needed to leave my house by 7:30 am, get in the shower by 7:00 am, and ensure my alarm went off by 6:45 am. The ride in the car often allowed me to "get ready" for my school day mentally and based on what I needed, each day looked different—sometimes a check on NPR to hear the news, sometimes a blasting of upbeat house or latin rock to wake me up, and sometimes my Pandora Sarah McLaughlin channel allowing me to sing my heart out. This routine helped me organize myself for the day ahead, and the flexibility allowed me to be responsive to my own needs, which often differed based on the day, the weather, and my prior night's sleep. Every educator I know has a similar cadence of routine—a regular time to awake, a morning routine that is predictable and follows a pattern, but some level of customization possible based on need. On a typical day, there were interruptions at times—a car accident delaying my regular route, a realization that I used the last coffee pod and I'd need to stop on my way to caffeinate my journey, or a child waking up with a fever. Due to my ability to recognize how each of these stressors impacted me, I was able to, in most cases, think rationally and manage my emotions to accomplish the task of getting to school on times and being ready to teach my students on a daily basis.

However, emergency remote teaching came on suddenly, without warning, and necessitated an immediate paradigm shift in the creation of daily routines as an educator. Again, due to the sudden nature, we were unable to prepare and organize ourselves for success. Because of this disruption and the emergency remote learning period that followed, many educators were unable to develop not only the emotional regulation skills but also the focus and persistence skills required for successful Self-Awareness and Self-Management. Therefore, it is critical that we take time to develop new routines and working norms for ourselves in our new "work" setting, as we experience and become aware of dysregulation. In order to do so, we advocate taking time to answer the following questions and clearly define the new routines and norms required in your home for successful Self-Awareness and Self-Management.

- ◆ Do I have a regular wake up and getting ready routine that prepares me for teaching?
- ◆ Do I have a consistent work space and place that signals to others in my home that I am "at work"?
- ◆ What is my routine for breaks? Who do I engage with and why?
- ◆ What is my ending the day routine? How do the others I live with know when I am "off the clock"?
- ◆ Do I need transition time between *work* and *home*? How can I achieve that when the physical environment overlaps?

We have never been advocates of the term *work-life balance* as it is impossible to achieve in many cases. However, ensuring that, as educators working in a virtual environment, we look to achieve successful work-life integration depending on the moment is critical to the development of our own intrapersonal SEL competencies. Virtual and remote teaching and learning has disrupted our routines. Ensuring we re-establish routines for the virtual environment is critical for success—not just for this space and place of remote learning, but to more easily respond and adapt to the new educational reality awaiting us in the future.

Good teaching is subject to compassion. Whether we are working with a student to tame their crippling fear of failure or if we are struggling to keep our cool when a challenging student pushes our buttons, our level of compassion toward our students can often be predicted by our level of compassion *toward ourselves*. Educators must model compassion toward themselves and their students. An educator's ability to be compassionate—toward themselves and their students—is something that is felt immediately upon entering their room—even if this room is a virtual classroom. It is a space where students feel seen with a compassionate lens. Negativity toward one student is often sensed by the rest of the class and erodes the climate and culture of the classroom. One student being unwelcome in a room does not make the others feel inherently *more* welcome. This can actually be more transparent in a virtual setting, where students can see and feel the emotions of some of the other students in the classroom who have their cameras on in a much deeper way, since the majority of the virtual classroom "environment" is taken up by the faces of the learners. A virtual classroom space that welcomes all, even those that test our patience, creates a consistent, emotionally resilient, and compassionate environment for learning—or, as Charlotte Danielson describes, an *environment of respect and rapport* in which students will feel they have the space to explore Self-Awareness without shame (Danielson & CPS, 2011).

School is equally a personal and interpersonal pursuit. To be successful, our students must learn to balance the needs of the self with the needs of the collective. The secret here is to explicitly teach the competencies without becoming the domineering narrator inside your students' heads. As former teachers, we knew many educators whose style was so prescriptive that there was no room for student Self-Awareness to be cultivated. Students never learn to be self-aware or to self-regulate, they simply learn to comply. This becomes even more extreme in a virtual setting, where connection is limited and to be successful, students need even more Self-Awareness and Self-Management than in the past (as do educators!). Therefore, it is clear that the virtual environment has enhanced our need to ensure that both students and staff work on well-being in all forms—now, their success in academics truly depends on it in every single way!

Connecting with Others: Interpersonal Emotional Intelligence (SOCIAL)

As humans, we are wired for connection—despite teaching in a remote setting, we still thrive on personal and professional connections with others. As teachers and professionals, this comes in the form of professional collaboration and socialization, as well as developing relationships with people outside of our homes and connecting with others to ensure accountability for self-care.

The emergency remote learning period also disrupted our regular way of acting and interacting with our colleagues, and developing relationships with others. Communication and ways to collaborate as well as our typical practicing of social skills as adults through regular interactions (think: staff meetings, hallway interactions, lunch in the teachers' lounge) has not only isolated us as individuals, but taken away many of the avenues by which we continually practiced our relationship skills and social awareness in an in-person setting. In addition to focusing on our Self-Awareness and Self-Management in this new setting, it is critical for us as educators to find new ways to develop these communication skills and attend to the practice of social interactions to continue to grow our perspective-taking, empathy, and recognition of issues of inequality so that we can be effective in our craft. This is what connection means in a virtual setting. Think about the following questions:

◆ What regular routines can you put in place to discuss student concerns, and collaborate with other staff to accomplish goals related to student learning?

◆ How do you effectively express your gratitude, needs or concerns in this new environment?

◆ Do you regularly engage in non-school related conversation with others during the work week both with school-based personnel and outside friends or neighbors?

◆ How comfortable are you being vulnerable and experiencing a range of emotions (laughing, crying, fear, excitement) with others both in and outside of your inner circle or immediate family?

◆ How have you shared in the different experiences of others during the pandemic? Have you engaged in self-inquiry or reflected upon your level of empathy and emotional availability?

Creating a plan for connection, both personal and professional, is a key driver of developing and practicing being an emotionally intelligent educator. The key here is recognizing and addressing the unique and inherent challenges that arise out of the physical isolation which occurs during any type of remote or virtual learning and making a plan to continually develop and practice your communication and social skills regardless of location.

Cultivating Relaxed Alertness: Cognitive Engagement in Teaching and Learning

A growing body of scientific research refers to the term *relaxed alertness* as the optimal state for learning. In order to grow this in our students, we must first learn to identify and cultivate it in ourselves as educators. Relaxed alertness is a state of being that can be temporary, but can also become a defining trait in adults or students. It is characterized by feelings of confidence, competence, and motivation grounded in meaning or purpose (Caine, Caine, McClintic, & Klimek, 2015). Many of these feelings were significantly disrupted as a result of the sudden onset of the emergency remote learning period, but also, have persisted into the virtual learning period we are currently in. In order to successfully navigate our own cognitive engagement in teaching and learning which results in positive decision making around the teaching and learning for our students in our virtual classrooms, we must self-reflect and connect to achieving this state as educators, so that we can effectively identify the diverse needs of our students and use this state to impact their ability to learn in this new setting.

Both children and adults in a state of relaxed alertness experience an environment of low threat and high challenge. In order to cultivate this state in our classrooms, we must first cultivate it in ourselves. Consider the following questions about your own work environment:

- ◆ Are you being equally challenged and supported in this new educational setting and with the new educational expectations?
- ◆ Do you experience excitement or fear with the new challenges ahead? Why?
- ◆ How do you manage uncertainty and ambiguity, with logic, grace, and a sense of inquiry?
- ◆ How does your administrator facilitate this state of being as an educator?

The Mindful Practices approach creates a state of relaxed alertness in educators so that they can take on the challenges that lie ahead in teaching and learning. This approach is closely aligned to the CASEL core SE competencies and clusters, defined as: *Social and emotional competence (SEC) is the capacity to coordinate cognition, affect, and behavior that allows individuals to thrive in diverse cultures and contexts and achieve specific tasks and positive developmental outcomes (Elias et al., 1994). . . . These clusters emphasize the importance of developing both intrapersonal competencies that include Self-Awareness and Self-Management and interpersonal competencies that include social awareness and relationship skills (CASEL, 2020).*

- ◆ **Self-Awareness:** The ability to understand one's own emotions, thoughts, and values and how they influence behavior across contexts. This includes capacity to recognize one's strengths and limitations with a well-grounded sense of confidence and purpose.
- ◆ **Self-Management:** The ability to manage one's emotions, thoughts, and behaviors effectively in different situations and to achieve goals and aspirations. This includes the capacity to delay gratification, manage stress, and feel motivation and agency to accomplish personal/collective goals.
- ◆ **Social Awareness:** The ability to understand the perspectives of and empathize with others, including those from diverse backgrounds,

cultures, and contexts. This includes the capacity to feel compassion for others, understand broader historical and social norms for behavior in different settings, and recognize family, school, and community resources and supports.

In these terms, the Mindful Practices SEL approach focuses on the following SEC clusters, with an added emphasis on the balance between Self-Efficacy and Social Harmony, as highlighted in the SELF (Intrapersonal) and SOCIAL (Interpersonal) practices:

- ◆ **Self-Awareness:** Building this competency cultivates an awareness of self, empowering the learner with the self-knowledge to better address their mental, emotional, and well-being needs.
- ◆ **Self-Regulation:** Building this competency constructs the bridge from awareness to regulation and can shift the learner from impulsivity to intentional navigation of behavioral choices.
- ◆ **Social Awareness:** Building this competency cultivates an awareness of self in social situations. What we bring into the room and how the energy and atmosphere in the room impacts us. By building this competency the learner can move from a reactive mindset to a more proactive, communal view of their role in the world around them.
- ◆ **Self-Efficacy and Social Harmony:** When in balance, the learner feels centered, present, and like a valued and contributing member of the world around them. This competency also reflects the learner's ability to find their voice and to balance the needs of the self with the needs of others, without projection, assumption, or excessive self-sacrifice.

Mindfulness is one of the vehicles Mindful Practices we use to create space for stillness of space to cultivate that bedrock, intrapersonal SE competency, Self-Awareness. This book examines the interplay between interpersonal and intrapersonal SEL skill development and how the practices of vocalization, movement, stillness, and teamwork, or what we call *Mindful Practices* develop not only one's Self-Awareness but, in turn, an increased ability for one to form positive human connections with others.

Taking a cue from Precious Jenning's work at Columbia College in Chicago, "Self-Awareness is cultivated by the union between the body and mind found within these four practices: vocalization, movement, stillness and human connection." (Philibert, 2022, p. 14)The goal of the POP Chart and the practices housed within is to utilize a mix of Mindful Practices to build Self-Awareness, Self-Regulation, and Social Awareness so that students can find the balance between Self-Efficacy and Social Harmony, and balancing the needs of the self and the needs of the collective.

- ◆ **Vocalization:** speaking, chanting, singing.
- ◆ **Movement:** gross/fine/locomotor, yoga, dance, fitness.
- ◆ **Stillness:** reflection, breath work, meditation.
- ◆ **Human Connection:** play, collaboration, communication.

Each of these four practices is experiential in nature and will resonate differently with each student or adult, as we all have different entry points to this work based upon myriad, individual factors such as exposure to trauma, physical mobility, or sleep intake. To meet students and adults at that entry point, the practice is not merely reading about the positive impacts of breath work or movement on the body. Instead, they practice while paying attention on purpose (mindfulness), and over time learn how their bodies respond, cultivating an understanding of what they need and when they need it (Self-Awareness).

With a POP Check, students (and/or adults) find a practice like journaling, yoga, or breathwork, to meet the needs of their bodies and minds at that moment in time. Over time, this continual, intentional practice of cultivating Self-Awareness empowers adults and children alike to read and respond proactively to their bodies' cues instead of feeling victimized by their own emotional reactions or moments of dysregulation.

When adults and students have the Self-Awareness to read and respond proactively to their bodies' cues they can act with agency, connect more authentically and engage in power sharing. One of objectives of SEL integration across a school building must be adults engaging in this intentional self-inquiry, so that they can better witness and reckon with their own SEC and how it impacts the climate and culture of their classrooms.

As discussed earlier, it is critical that time is allotted not only for educators to develop their SEC, but for them to begin with and spend ample time on Self-Awareness, the bedrock of the Social Emotional competences. When educators develop their Self-Awareness, they better understand their own lenses and biases and have the tools to move beyond defining a student by a single story that they may or may not be reacting to in the present moment.

Development of educator Self-Awareness is critical for the anti-racist work that, together with well-being and SEL, must be inextricable from the fabric of how schools operate. For anti-racist work to be authentically implemented in schools, educators must encourage students to become agents of change, allowing for their voices and perspectives to be seen and heard. Educators and students act differently when they have agency and feel they can make a difference in the landscape of the school environment, without relinquishing power or sacrificing self-identity. They are able to build the relational trust needed to co-create and inform the climate and culture of a classroom, because they have the awareness to manage and understand their emotions, reactions, and needs and the energy they are bringing into the environment itself.

We will use the subsequent chapters of this text to redesign and realign these practices to the virtual environment and prepare ourselves as educators for a new educational environment that will likely forever integrate in-person and virtual modes.

2

Creating the Climate and Conditions for a Socio-Emotionally Healthy Virtual Classroom

We all know students learn best when they feel welcomed, comfortable, and safe. A virtual classroom and school culture is more than Zoom Happy Hours, scavenger hunts, and dress up days. It's a space where each student and teacher feels comfortable, safe, respected, and treated like a valued member of the classroom and school; it's where they feel like they belong. When the student leaves a school (and the community that knows their SEL needs) and moves on to the new environment (where their SEL needs are unknown), they are often unsuccessful. This can even be true with a change in mode of instruction, even when the teacher and the class environment changes (i.e. with an emergency closure, intermittent need for remote teaching and learning, etc.). A student might know that they "liked the way that their old classroom operated," but they are not empowered with the Self-Awareness or the words to voice their needs as new environments present themselves. Transparency and opportunities for voice are key for students to take ownership of the SEL process and find agency as learners. As John Hattie notes in *Visible Learning* (2009), educators modeling and discussing SEL strategies in real time is one of the most impactful implementation methods, as it promotes student agency and ownership. Hattie also notes that social skill training should be provided regularly and for the duration of the school year at least one time per week. Additionally, measured, predictable, and consistent delivery must take place over time, as Catherine Cook-Cottone's work (2015) around "dosage" demonstrates.

This is why significant and devoted attention is paid to creating the climate and conditions in the virtual classroom, similar to the necessary time

DOI: 10.4324/9781003183204-3

needed to creating climate and conditions for effective in-person learning at the beginning of the school year. Similar to the assertions made in the previous chapter about adult needs, students thrive on routine and predictability—much of which is removed in the virtual setting. Simply taking the Class Agreements and systems for self and social management from the in-person classroom into the virtual setting is necessary, but not sufficient. These systems and procedures need to take on a new life, specific to the virtual world, in order to exhibit similar success as when in-person learning was the norm. Why is this the case? Well, simply put, because there are more and different distractions in the virtual environment, less control of the environment by the teacher and different ways to identify and measure engagement than when all students are present in the same setting—the classroom.

Distractions in a Virtual Classroom

The quantity and variability of distractions for students in a virtual setting increases exponentially from those distractions in the in-person classroom. This is because students not only have to deal with what is in their own home setting, but also that which they experience virtually in 20 different households represented by their classmates. Consider the following example: Gaby is a third grader who has her own room, desk and her school computer in her bedroom for synchronous learning time. While her teacher is doing the morning announcements she looks over at the side of her bookcase where her fish tank is. She thinks, "I don't remember if I fed my fish Blue this morning . . . did I?" Then her teacher calls on her to share her response to the daily edit. Gaby is flustered, embarrassed, and not sure how to respond.

This is just one example, but consider the following additional possibilities, all of which we have observed occur during the emergency remote learning period with teachers and students with whom we work:

◆ *Additional siblings working near or in the same room at the same time, but in a different subject area (think one student in physical education class and the other in math)*
◆ *Parents on their own work calls*
◆ *Books, toys, a bed, an open window, peeling paint, a falling picture—all visual distractions from the task at hand*
◆ *Internet outages, interruptions, breakages, etc.*
◆ *Feeling hungry and knowing the kitchen is next door*
◆ *Hearing the doorbell ring*
◆ *Hearing your pet bark or meow, needing attention*
◆ *Seeing or hearing other students' pets, siblings, doorbells during on screen time*

This chapter will take many of the typical successful in-classroom Mindful Practices' structures and help educators adjust them for the virtual setting to ensure a healthy and safe classroom culture and community, even in the virtual space.

The components outlined here are invaluable components of your SEL Classroom These concepts should be pre-taught and re-taught to help guarantee student success. *Teacher cues for each activity are in italic type, for ease of implementation.*

- **Thumb Check and POP Chart** *A practice to ensure students have space to own their feelings through Self-Awareness, recognize and express their needs, and build a strong, interpersonal relationship with a caring adult*
- **Sample Implementation Schedule** *To help teachers create a consistent, safe, and impactful classroom*
- **Classroom Agreements** *A list of guidelines to explicitly frame expectations*
- **Talking Stick** *An indigenous practice to ensure equity of voice during whole group discussion*

Intentionality is key to impactful SEL implementation. When done well, this intentional implementation positively impacts a classroom's climate and culture. An observer can see it, hear it, and feel it as soon as they enter the room. The POP Chart gives students space to Pause (breathe and be still), Own it (name their emotions/feelings), and Practice (a solution) so that students are given the tools to deal with their *legitimate concerns* to keep learning. This is even more critical in a virtual setting, where there is less teacher observation and direct oversight and a higher need for students to engage in Self-Management to be successful throughout the school day.

Some key questions to consider before implementation:

- What time each day will your students use or reference the POP Chart? Will this occur during synchronous or asynchronous time? How can this system be set up for successful implementation with teacher oversight and during independent learning time?
- When will you use a quick Thumb Check with your students? Will it be physical, use of the reactions bar on the screen, or a private chat message? When would you implement each of these options and why?
- What do you do if your class needs a reset or your students need additional support?

All Hands On Deck

Thumb Checks are a quick and simple way to give students an opportunity to assess their own feelings and body sensations in the moment, and for the educators, and students, to get a measure of the students' feelings. We recommend that all school stakeholders check in with students as they start their days in the virtual setting. This can occur as students enter the virtual classroom with a physical thumb representation, or with an emoji sent directly to the teacher only in the chat, so that he/she can cue students to go to the POP Chart if they need an activity to reset. In the virtual setting, students should have regular access to the POP Chart if needed at all times—either as a separate part of their School Management System (Google Classroom or Schoology for example), or to be able to utilize the Mindful Practices' SEL on Demand portal in order for students to self-select activities that can help them reset to start or continue their days.

The wonderful thing about a Thumb Check is that it is a tool that an entire school staff can use quickly and easily to check in with students, whether they are in or out of the classroom. For instance, from 7:45 am to 7:55 am, while the principal is leading the morning announcements and Pledge of Allegiance for the whole school virtually—either live or recorded, staff of all types—administrators, deans, social workers, parent volunteers, custodians, and lunchroom staff could be reviewing students Thumb Checks in the chat boxes, or identifying potential students of concern and signaling them to check the chat, or join a quick breakout session to reset and get ready for the day ahead. This all hands on deck approach utilizes all caring adults in the community and communicates to students that nothing—answering emails, being on the phone, entering grades, texting, or squeezing in that last bit of lesson planning—trumps the importance of being present and emotionally available for the students. It is a shared expectation for each and every adult in the building, encouraging students to build lasting interpersonal relationships with caring adults who are not necessarily their classroom teacher. This also gives school stakeholders a chance to help support students across their school experience. "Hi, Ms. Jimenez. I connected with Takia as she entered the virtual classroom this morning. She mentioned she is having a Thumbs-Down day. I know that you coach her in soccer and that you two have a great relationship. Do you mind checking in with her later during your virtual practice?"

Some questions to ask yourself in order to successfully adapt this practice to the virtual setting are as follows: What are non-classroom based staff doing to start their day in our school? How can I engage some of the educational support personnel (secretaries, assistants, specials teachers, administrators, janitors) in my morning routines so that we can utilize our "all hands on deck" approach, even during short or long bursts of remote learning? If only some students are learning remotely, how can this "all hands on deck" approach assist in facilitating school connectedness at a deeper level for those students learning virtually?

Thumb Check

At multiple points throughout the day or instructional period, an educator may ask students for a quick *Thumb Check*. The purpose of a Thumb Check is first and foremost to build interpersonal relationships between students and adults through the consistent practice of processing and sharing feelings. It is also a practical tool to gauge students' energy or emotions. The educator simply signals the students to hold their thumbs against their chests, which is quick and easy if the class is transitioning between activities, or if a student is interacting with a teacher one-on-one. In the virtual classroom, this can be an actual physical thumb, an emoji representation publicly, or a private chat to the teacher if a student wants to keep their "Thumb Check" private.

Thumbs-Up = I'm experiencing pleasant feelings: calm, relaxed, happy
Thumbs to the Side = Meh. I'm bored, restless, distracted
Thumbs-Down = I'm experiencing unpleasant feelings: sad, mad, stressed, hungry

Giving your students multiple methods to check in demonstrates that you are invested in providing opportunities for all your students to practice naming, identifying, and proactively acknowledging their emotions. This takes on an even greater significance in the virtual environment as educators cannot directly observe student behavior, out of view stimuli or the entirety of a reaction a student might be having to something inside or outside the classroom. Therefore, providing even *more* opportunities for these quick Self-Awareness opportunities is critical in the virtual setting for all students, but especially for those students who may have significant challenges with the alternative mode of teaching and learning.

Additionally, encourage all school stakeholders, parents, administrators, staff, and community members to check in with students as part of the morning greeting and at any point over the course of the school day with a quick Thumb Check. Additionally, empower your Thumbs-Down students to be the solution and select an activity from the POP Chart to help positively shift their energy so that they can be attentive and present learners. Some students may consistently display a Thumbs-Down just for the attention it garners. Do not dismiss a Thumbs-Down signal; however, this can be a great window into a valuable conversation with a learner in need. These conversations can happen in a breakout room, in a private chat box, or at an asynchronous time for virtual learners.

Starting the Day with a POP Check

Those educators with a classroom and bulletin board space can move beyond a Thumb Check to a POP Chart. As the students enter your virtual classroom, give them two minutes of music to get their materials organized and visit the **POP Chart**. Especially if these tools have already been used in the in-person learning classroom, modifying these procedures for the virtual setting can have an added impact for remote learners. POP Charts can exist virtually in a slide deck the teacher provides, a virtual wall provided within the school management system, or teachers can even create individual POP Charts that are sent home to students to display in their homes for individual use on and offline.

Use Jamboard, a Whiteboard in Google Meets, Ideaboarz, Mural, or other free screen sharing website as you enter your virtual classroom each morning. As part of the morning routine, each student moves their picture (or if you have had students create their own bitmoji this can be a fun way to integrate classroom use of these virtual pictures) to the appropriate place on the chart: Thumbs-Up, Thumbs to the Side, or Thumbs-Down. As the music plays, students **PAUSE** to check in with how they are feeling. Then, they **OWN IT** by moving their picture to indicate their emotions or feelings. Lastly, they choose an activity to **PRACTICE** in their home workspace that will help them be present for instruction.

> **Pause:** Stop for a moment and take a deep breath. What are you thinking? What are you experiencing?
> **Own It:** Name your emotions and feelings, "I am Frustrated," "I am Anxious," "I am Happy," etc.
> **Practice:** Find the practice that can help you be present, focused, and ready to learn.

For those individual students that have moved their picture or bitmoji to indicate they are having a difficult day, find a time during instruction to connect with that student in a breakout room, via the chat box or other mode, and offer a SEL or mindfulness practice that would meet their needs. Sometimes, they just might need to connect with an adult. Ask permission to extend a virtual hug or five, or find a little time to chit-chat.

It is recommended that the educator set clear expectations with students, to help ensure that the POP Chart Check-In routine is a smooth, fluid, and safe process. Whole-class implementation (Tier 1) is preferred, with extended time in the POP Chart for students with exceptionalities or who need assistance modifying their behavior throughout the day.

Protocols and Procedures

Once the POP Chart has been set up, it is important to take the time to walk students through their routine prior to implementation, as the student check-ins will take place during non-instructional time (before academics begin). Although simple, model the strategies for the students, demonstrating how to perform a Thumb Check, use an activity in the POP Chart, etc. As Harry Wong points out in his *Facilitator's Handbook* (2009), consistently practiced classroom routines at the start of the school year can be the key to student success, regardless of the age. As one of the goals of the POP Check is to build the interpersonal relationship between the student and teacher, reinforce an emotionally and physically safe virtual classroom environment by being transparent and consistent.

Anytime a new activity is learned, a text box with the new practice should be added to the POP Chart to serve as a reminder for students that they can access these regulatory strategies at any time. If you have sent individual physical POP Charts home, students can create their own cards to add to their charts when new skills and strategies are learned. To build student ownership of the POP Chart, encourage them to suggest activities that they have tried outside of your class, and to utilize their own pictures, language, and visuals that will help them to independently use the strategies when needed.

Post procedures for taking a break next to the POP Chart. Clearly establish your expectations for POP Chart behavior (i.e., Can students turn off their camera and indicate to the teacher that they are using the POP Chart? Are there any times when the POP Chart is closed?)

Step 1 Ensure the virtual timer is set for three minutes. Students should start the timer when they begin their POP Check break.
Step 2: Choose an activity to practice from the POP Chart.
Step 3: When the timer goes off, stop the activity and return to the activity at hand.

Create a Comfortable Space

The POP Chart can be a place for a student to be alone with their thoughts, or to reset when they need a moment to get centered. Because our typical materials like comfortable bean bags, cushions, and pillows are not always available in learner's homes, create a soothing background that students can access in their virtual setting in order to replicate this restful, relaxing place to reset. If possible, ask students to create their own comfortable spaces physically in their homes. However, this is not necessary. Students can utilize supplies sent from school including: art supplies, colored pencils and plain scratch paper. Because you cannot create your typical basket of books with positive quotations and affirmations, you can create these quotations in your virtual setting, or be sure that links to websites with these positive affirmations are available for students when needed.

Given the importance of a positive and collaborative climate and culture, *the following educator scripts in italic type* help you utilize the Thumb Check or POP Chart to bring your classroom back together to a centered, present, and compassionate place.

Frenetic Energy

It is the week before Winter Break and the teacher notices her class is unusually frenetic. Instead of using shaming language such as "I cannot believe what a crazy class we are today!" the teacher recruits the students' help in finding a solution to set her class up for a successful group work activity.

*OK, Room [x], I notice we have a lot of extra energy this morning. Let's use a relaxation activity to help us be present and focused. [Student name] what activity from our **POP Chart** do you think could help us get centered? [Student responds.* Teacher facilitates activity.] *Nicely done, class. Before we get back to work, I would like to get a quick **Thumb Check** from our room.* [Students hold thumbs up to chest, teacher takes a moment to process where the energy of the class is and whether they need another activity or are ready to continue with their assignment.] *Thank you, class. It looks like we are ready to continue our lesson.*

Worried Students

The school has extended remote learning for a month and the teacher knows her students would benefit from a bit of yoga or physical movement to help process feelings of stress and anxiety.

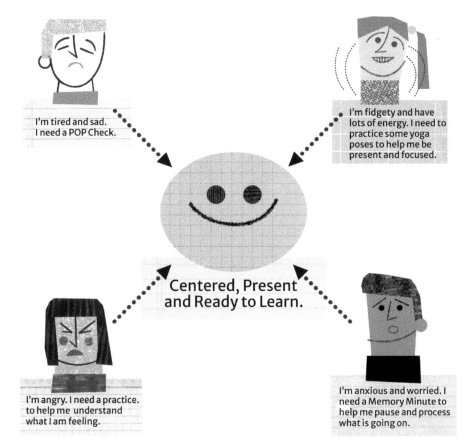

Figure 2.1 Students in an SEL-Informed Classroom

*I know we all anticipated returning to school next week and it is certainly a letdown to receive the news that our remote learning period has been extended. I noticed that most students entered class today and put their bitmoji/picture next to 'Meh' on the **POP Chart**. Thank you for sharing your feelings. I care about you and want to do all I can to help our class with our worries. [Student x], please lead our class through your favorite POP Chart activity, to help us combat feelings of anxiety that we may be experiencing.*

Withdrawn Learners

Room [x], I notice our energy is low, and we still have our projects to complete today. Let's use an SEL activity to energize ourselves. [Student name], can you name a **POP Chart** activity that will help energize our class and stimulate our brains? [Student leads the class through the selected activity.] *Nicely done, Room [x]. Before we transition, I would like to get a quick* **Thumb Check** *from our room.* [Students hold thumbs up to chest, enter emoji in text box or otherwise indicate their Thumb Check virtually, the teacher takes a moment to process where the energy of the class is and whether they need another activity or are ready to continue with their assignment.] *Thank you, class. Now, we are ready to get to work.*

Solo POP Chart Check-ins

You can cue a student at any point throughout your class to utilize a POP Chart activity, if they need to take a moment to reset. Honor where students are with both mood and energy and move them toward a state of relaxed alertness.

> *Sun-Hi, I noticed you are having a difficult time focusing. Would one of our POP Chart practices help you regulate your behavior? If so, how much time do you think you would need before returning to work with your group on the project?*

A process like this can empower a student with the choice and agency that comes with cultivating Self-Awareness and Self-Regulation skills, instead of simply disciplining them for being off task or not engaged. It is important that the student owns the shift in their energy, not the educator who casually observes, "OK, fine. It looks like you are x, y or z." Even if it takes a bit more effort, try your best to give your students the space to understand their emotions and how to regulate them, not what *you think* they may be experiencing.

Ultimately, especially in the virtual setting, the goal is for students to understand the process and procedure and self-select to engage in a POP Check in order to successfully re-engage in the synchronous class learning, or continue and persist through the asynchronous work activities.

This is why checking-in daily with the POP Chart becomes a daily component of a classroom routine, even in a virtual setting. Instead of reacting to student behavior or merely managing a class, a teacher facilitates shame-free opportunities for students to cultivate Self-Awareness and learn how to regulate. Often, we have observed virtual classrooms skipping these critical components in favor of more time focused on academic instruction. However, it is clear that when students do not feel safe and ready to learn, the academic learning they experience is useless. Therefore, we highly encourage a deep reflection by each educator on these elements in order to ensure students can get the most out of their academic learning time.

By defining what is *managing* your students' behavior (i.e. classroom management, classroom consequences, etc.) and what is SEL (i.e. giving students the space and agency to develop their own Self-Awareness and Self-Regulation skills so that they can *manage* their own behavior), educators create a clearly defined set of expectations and routines. An educator approaches student issues consistently and predictably from the vantage point of an ally wanting to assist in the growth of their Self-Awareness, not the authority figure whose rules may change day to day based upon mood. The SEL-informed educator sets clear and consistent expectations. And, instead of being emotionally reactive or shaming when those expectations are not met, has the Self-Awareness to realize that they may be triggered, pauses to take a breath and works with the student to seek prevention out of awareness.

Talking Stick

Some of the teachers we work with feature the *POP Chart* and *Talking Stick* as central components of the fabric of their classrooms. Talking Stick is an indigenous practice utilizing a passed object to facilitate equity of voice. In the in-person setting, the student who is holding the stick gets to speak while the other students are active and engaged listeners. Although this is a simple principle, we recommend crafting Agreements to guarantee that this activity is equitable for all. These Agreements can extend to general sharing, circle time, or large group discussions. Obviously, a talking stick cannot be used when students are separated by location, and using a talking stick may not be appropriate due to regulations around shared equipment and materials for some time in schools. However, it is critical that there is a method in your classroom to ensure that air time is shared throughout synchronous class time, and there is an intentional way of indicating for students that they would like to engage in a conversation or activity.

Ensuring Student Participation in the Virtual Setting

Students in virtual classrooms face a myriad of additional challenges and opportunities when it comes to participating in group conversations and using protocols for engagement. There are additional stimuli and distractions at home—from siblings in close spaces on different classes to pets to doorbells and deliveries. It is helpful for students to self-identify these distractions, and share them with the class if they are able. This helps others stay engaged when similar distractions may occur. For example, Joey keeps glancing over to his fish during a teacher directed lesson. He stands up while on camera, goes over, feeds the fish, and seems generally distracted during the lesson as he is overly focused on his pet fish, Blue. Joey has shared many times about Blue to the class. As the teacher notices Joey's focus on Blue, she needs to ensure that she both re-engages Joey in the classroom content, but also acknowledges his need to connect with his pet. She can send him a private chat or give him a chance to briefly turn off his camera, take a break with Blue, and come back using a timer on screen. Whatever the teacher does, we want to ensure that she does not "call out" Joey [think: "Joey, I notice you are distracted by Blue, please return to the class"], but rather provides him an opportunity to self-identify the why behind his distraction, and find a way on his own to re-engage with the class. Typically in class, potentially, she would give him the option of going to the Peace Place or the Calm Down Corner, but that's not an option in the virtual setting. Turning a camera off, or using a breakout room can be just this break that a student may need to get back into the mindset of learning. Consider how many times you've used the "call out" option rather than the Self-Management option for students, especially in the virtual setting, and how you could think through a change in this action?

It is recommended that you visually display your Talking Stick Agreements and place them next to the POP Chart in your virtual classroom. While each grade level is different, below are a few essential steps for creating your Talking Stick Agreements:

◆ The student with the selected emoji is the only one to speak.
◆ The Talking Stick is passed silently from student to student (often in a circle). In the virtual setting, teachers should set up the way in which the emoji will be transferred from student to student (often using a randomly ordered student list that is displayed so that students can anticipate their turn).
◆ Pre-teach listening expectations for a Talking Stick session. What does active listening look like and sound like in this setting? For example: how do we exhibit listening skills if our cameras are on? What if our cameras are off? How can we engage and ensure the speaker is validated and recognized?
◆ Students must wait until each student has had a chance to share before they request to speak again. The teacher should let the students know that there may not be enough time for everyone to have

another turn. Alternatively, students can choose to "pass" any time. (Note: this is especially critical in the virtual setting. Students can "hide" more easily or might not as easily engage in activities since they are not physically present.)

◆ The speaker must use "I" language and talk only about their experiences.

◆ The teacher should conclude the Talking Stick activity with a Thumb Check, before transitioning to the next activity.

Crafting General Classroom Agreements

Crafting Class Agreements and norms for students takes on a new challenge and opportunity in the virtual setting. As previously discussed, the significant amount of additional stimuli present in the home environment multiplies the impact of potential distractions that take away from learning. It is generally understood that communities should craft and retain three to five Agreements (notice the use of the term Agreements rather than "class rules"). This is so that students can identify and internalize the most important habits and dispositions they should maintain in the classroom setting. Additionally, Agreements should be stated in the affirmative (rather than the negative— "don't do this"), specific and constructed using student voice and agency. One way to do this is to have students reflect on in-school Agreements and engage in a conversation about adjusting them for a new environment. Another way is to begin with sample Agreements for students to reflect upon. Below are sample Agreements to use as a platform to build consensus among your students about shared experience in your classroom. The Agreements help students craft their virtual school experience with voice and agency. The Agreements should be signed by all class members, both adults and teachers, and posted next to the POP Chart. In the virtual setting, students can "sign" by creating another visual image surrounding the Agreements that lives inside the virtual classroom on a daily basis, either within the management system or as a slide to begin each and every day.

Sample Agreements
1. Check-in with a Thumb Check.
2. Use the POP Chart and Talking Stick.
3. Follow the Speaker with your Eyes, whether you are on camera or not.
4. Use the chat feature to connect with the teacher and express your needs.
5. Use and respect Teacher and Classmates Signals (Clap Reactions and Thumbs Down; Snaps and Table Taps in-person).

Through the creation of Class Agreements in the virtual space, respect for each other and the learning community is reinforced. Teacher action then needs to compliment these Agreements. Consider for a moment the following actions and how they reinforce or contradict the Class Agreements:

- ◆ Many students share at once so the teacher "mutes" all students
- ◆ Chat function is disabled without reason stated
- ◆ Teacher publicly calls out students whose cameras are off

Virtual learning is a new endeavor that is here to stay in one form or another. It is important that we take a look at our practices and automatic reactions as educators and critically analyze how they align or conflict with the safe classroom space we hope to create—both virtually and in-person.

★ **Teacher Tip:** Clap reactions = students use the reaction bar at the bottom of the screen to indicate claps when they agree with the student speaking Thumbs down = students use this reaction when someone breaks an agreement or says something disrespectful either in the chat or verbally.

Sample Charts: Observable SEL Student Behavior in a Virtual Setting

Table 2.1 Examples of behaviors that can be observed in a virtual setting

Self-Awareness: Body Awareness and Personal Responsibility	
Does look like or sound like	**Does NOT look like or sound like**
• Making healthy lifestyle choices (drinking water or eating a healthy snack when necessary) • Having fidgits nearby to minimize time off camera and utilizing them appropriately but not as a distraction to self or others	• Making unhealthy lifestyle choices (drinking soda onscreen or eating sweets or chips during class) • Making faces on camera and pointing at someone's new hairdo or clothing

Self-Regulation : Expressing Emotions and Managing Stress, Anger, and Anxiety	
Does look like or sound like	**Does NOT look like or sound like**
• Participating in the daily "Thumb Check" authentically • Utilizing our POP Chart throughout class to honor where you are and get what you need • Respecting our Agreements	• Distracting others and/or pretending to talk to the class • Eye-rolling, grunting or making comments under your breath or in the chat • Breaking our Agreements
Social Awareness: Active Listening and Service Orientation	
Does look like or sound like	**Does NOT look like or sound like**
• Respecting others' feelings, emotions, and opinions so that all voices can be heard • Honoring individual needs, spaces, and places	• Pointing at or pointing out distractions in your home or others' homes during class • Making negative comments like "that's stupid" or "what a dumb idea!" • Dominating the group with your voice • Speaking negatively or making assumptions about others' races or cultures

The balance between Self-Efficacy and Social Harmony (or, the duality between the intrapersonal and the interpersonal) is achieved when teachers and students build competency by working through the stages of Self-Awareness, Self-Regulation, and Social Awareness. Our model places Self-Awareness as the precursor to Self-Regulation, as we must be aware of a behavior in order to regulate it. That being said, because the contexts in which we live our lives are constantly shifting, the journey of the self, progressing from basic needs onward, is hardly linear. The emphasis here is on the balance between the *intrapersonal* and *interpersonal*, as school necessitates that learners balance the needs of the individual ("I want to get an A on this chemistry test!") with the challenges of the collective ("But I can't concentrate because Sarita's dog keeps barking, which is giving me a headache. I want to yell at her but I know my teacher will mute me. But, the teacher isn't doing anything about it because he is too busy helping another student who is still stuck on problem number 4. Really!?"). School is an intrapersonal pursuit housed within an interpersonal construct. To be an effective student, learners must astutely juggle both sets of needs.

Identifying SEL Competencies and Monitoring them Virtually

Progress monitoring of these SEL competencies, the same way we would for academic content, is key. However, because students' contexts are constantly shifting and changing, we should use caution when looking at mastery of SEL competencies as the primary outcome. Dr. Kiljoong Kim at Chapin Hall at the University of Chicago, our research partner, has studied the impact of the Mindful Practices model on both adult and student SEL skill development, as well as the importance of student voice and agency in this process. In his research he found that,

> Similar to mathematics, a student can perform computation when presented as is, but is unable to perform that same computation in a word problem. That is, one can display mastery of self-awareness but may not be able to apply that same self-awareness in different contexts. This doesn't mean that measuring mastery is useless, it means that self-awareness needs to be explored in varying contexts (among friends, during a test, outside of school, etc.) and, when possible, expressed in the learner's own words. (Instead of an adult trying to guess what a student is feeling or expressing.) Knowing the level of mastery of an SEL competency is helpful in that it can often tell you whether that student is ready to expand their level of exposure, or not.
>
> (Philibert, 2021, pp. 109–111)

Therefore, instead of mastery as the primary end goal, the goal of progress monitoring becomes agency—to give the learner (whether an adult or child) an increased awareness of their own skill development via practice over time. This process is and can be different for early childhood students and high school students, and so we recommend that educators create continued opportunities for students to cultivate voice and agency through consistent, developmentally appropriate opportunities for practice.

Teachers as learners should also reflect on the progress they are making on integrating these SEL competencies throughout their virtual learning environments. After a morning session or an academic lesson, teachers can create and use a checklist similar to the following to monitor their own progress on these SEL competencies.

Table 2.3 Self-Assessment checklist for teacher reflections on the inclusion of SEL competencies in virtual lessons

Self-Awareness	• Did I use positive facial gestures (smiles, thumbs up) throughout the lesson?
Self-Regulation	• Was I able to redirect attention from any distractions to the task at hand or did I participate (for example, by laughing at someone's dog?)
Social Awareness	• Did I acknowledge student participation did I use names only as a correction?

Taking Stock and Getting Started with the Activities

The SEL activities are broken up in the upcoming chapters by competency, like Self-Awareness. Please be mindful that students respond differently to movement and stillness strategies depending on their mental and emotional needs as well as their exposure to trauma. Although the chapters are segmented by SEL competency, there are activities included in each chapter that span grades K-12, and can be modified for a specific grade band.

The activities are either written as extended scripts, which include classroom management cues and pacing suggestions, or are written simply as activities (often as sequences), to be read aloud by the teacher or implemented as directed. *Scripted material is in italic type throughout the book.*

As we have mentioned in other areas of this book, we are not fans of scripted material being the main delivery vehicle for practitioners, as it does not build teacher SEL competency or encourage reflection. The intention behind the design of the scripted activities is to give the educator a vehicle with which to learn the delivery, pacing, and classroom management style that best complements the content. Given the length, the scripts are **not** designed to be read aloud to the students. Instead, it is recommended the teacher read through the scripts a few times to get a full picture of what the delivery looks, sounds, and feels like so that an emotionally and virtually safe space is created for the instruction to take place. Once the practitioner has mastered the pacing and classroom management cues, the POP Chart becomes a living, functioning element of the teacher's virtual classroom and the student's remote learning environment, meeting both student and teacher needs throughout the school day.

Using the Agreements and building consensus around the activity is important, not just to build an emotionally and virtually safe environment, but also so that the teacher can gain feedback from the students on why they believe they are practicing this skill and what the goal of the activity is. Each lesson contains a cue to "Give the students the 'Why' of the activity," to help build student ownership of the material and to empower them with the SEL knowledge to find their words, name emotions, and be in control of their behavior.

These practices are designed for universal, whole-class implementation (Tier I), not only for a few Tier II/III students to implement on their own or only with a social worker. Once the POP Chart is established, the activities should become part of your class check-in routine during their non-instructional time. The teacher may cue students who need help controlling their behavior to visit the POP Chart for a few minutes before returning to class, or the teacher may proactively insert a practice into the school day to help positively shift student energy toward being present. This can include 1:1 time, connecting in a breakout room or other individualized work with students during an intervention block to plan for ongoing engagement in the classroom environment. For students with exceptionalities, offer extended time in the POP Chart area and include activity modifications to guarantee inclusivity. Offer students an opportunity to join a few minutes early to get ready to learn and then stay on a few minutes at the end to ensure they can be self-directed in their asynchronous time, and have individualized time for questions. Creating an emotionally and virtually safe and accessible classroom environment is crucial for program implementation to be inclusive for all.

3

Self-Awareness and Self-Regulation
Activities to Promote Reflection and Self-Management Virtually

The practices within this chapter are designed to give students the space to cultivate SEL competencies, namely Self-Awareness and Self-Regulation. Self-Awareness is having the ability to understand your thoughts and emotions in addition to knowing how those factors influence your behavior. The World Health Organization recognizes Self-Awareness as one of ten life skills that promote well-being across all cultures. Self-Regulation comes after Self-Awareness, since to regulate one's emotions and actions, you must have awareness of them first. According to Hattie (2018), fostering student Self-Regulation is crucial for moving learning to deep and transfer levels.

After each practice has been taught, it should be added to the list of activities in your POP Chart, so that students can utilize it during their check-in routine or if they request a break during class or need to reframe themselves during asynchronous learning.

The majority of the practices in this chapter are written as scripted lessons for educators. This is to help educators learn both new content and a new instructional style. These scripts are *written in italic type* for ease of implementation and are labelled **Educator Script** in bold at the top of the page.

To build practitioner competency, we highly suggest reading the scripted practices and reframing them in your own words. Be mindful of implicit bias when teaching the lesson and make the time to see all students through a trauma-informed lens.

DOI: 10.4324/9781003183204-4

Self-Awareness and Self-Reflection in Early Childhood and Elementary School

Early childhood and elementary years are characterized by significant learning about self and rapid brain development. Therefore, it is critical that early childhood and elementary educators focus on implementing and practicing skills with students that build to successful Self-Regulation.

The awareness piece is exactly that—simply recognizing feelings, mood, or emotions and labelling them. The level of sophistication in doing this— recognizing and labeling emotions, feelings and resulting behaviors, grows significantly in the early childhood and elementary periods. And, just as children grow and develop physically at different rates, their emotional growth and development, including Self-Awareness and Self-Regulation, grows at differing rates too. Awareness is key as you cannot regulate (or control) behaviors that you do not recognize. Self-Regulation is the process that students' brains go through that gives them the ability to control their behaviors and emotions in response to a particular situation. For example, this means finding ways to cope with strong feelings so they don't become overwhelming; learning to focus and pay attention to different stimuli at different times; and, ultimately, successfully controlling behaviors required to get along with others and work in a community. Supporting the development of Self-Regulation in early childhood is an investment in later success, because stronger Self-Regulation predicts better performance in school, better relationships with others, and fewer behavioral difficulties (Rosanbalm & Murray, 2017).

During the preschool years, children experience rapid growth in areas of the brain associated with Self-Regulation, which makes them developmentally much more prepared to learn and use Self-Regulation skills. Concurrently, students are growing language skills during the preschool years that enable them to use words in managing their thoughts and feelings and asking for help. In this section, we will provide activities that support the growth of Self-Awareness and Self-Regulation skills through cultivating warm, responsive teacher/student relationships, intentionally structuring the virtual setting and teaching, and practicing specific skills that even young children can use independently. Early childhood and elementary students will need significant repetition, practice, and prompting, so teaching, re-teaching, and practicing these lessons repeatedly is common.

A note for teachers: adult modeling during this period of rapid brain development takes on significant importance as students watch their teachers closely to learn how they will behave. This includes how you as a teacher respond to unpredictable situations that may arise—with students or with other adults, and your reactions. Take note over the next week on how you react—both verbally and in non-verbal ways—to student behavior, interactions with other staff, or even small things that happen in your personal setting and how they impact your actions and interactions. What if you unexpectedly run out of coffee in your home? What if your internet is choppy? How you react and interact as a result of these unexpected issues has a direct result on your students' ability to develop Self-Awareness and implement Self-Regulation strategies in the classroom setting and beyond.

Self-Awareness and Self-Reflection in Middle School and High School

Middle school and high school students have very distinct needs in the areas of Self-Awareness and Self-Regulation. Students in these age ranges become more aware of the stimuli around them, and need extra practice and skill building in successfully managing self, many times, in order to successfully navigate peer and adult relationships. During this period, students also do grow at significantly individualized rates, providing a challenge for educators in dealing with the wide range of both emotional and physical development in their students. Self-Awareness and Self-Reflection in middle school and high school in a virtual setting takes on a new set of challenges for students in time-management and self-advocacy skills.

Given that middle school students typically see multiple teachers throughout the day, we strongly recommend sharing those practices that you feel are most successful with your colleagues. Continuity of approach, messaging, and practices between educators across a grade band or grade level can greatly increase the positive impact on your students overall, and strengthen their ability to use Self-Awareness and Self-Regulation skills to positively impact their classroom performance, and their engagement in school.

During virtual learning, there is a general tendency by educators, especially at the middle and high school level when synchronous learning time is significantly diminished, to focus exclusively on academic content needed for success. Educators should reframe this assumption and have students practice the following activities to continually develop SEL skills, even in a virtual setting. Self-Awareness and Self-Regulation takes on new importance for middle and high school students in the virtual setting because most of the time, the way that these students practice these skills is through regulating interactions with others, most of which is taken away in the virtual setting. Therefore, teachers should be deliberate in finding ways for students to continually practice this skill development across the curriculum.

Draw/Write and Rip

✓ Educator Script

Supplies:

- ◆ Icon to add the activity to the POP Chart or printable for students to add to their individual POP Chart at home.
- ◆ Music
- ◆ Scratch paper
- ◆ Recycling bin or garbage can
- ◆ Clock or timer

Time: 10 minutes

The Why Behind the Activity: *Today, we are practicing **Write and Rip**. We can practice Write and Rip during school at synchronous or asynchronous times or anytime we feel sad or something is bothering us at home.*

I have already created an icon for Write and Rip and added it to our POP Chart [Note: if you are using a virtual POP Chart, an icon works, if you have had each child set up their POP Chart at home, make sure they have access to an extra notecard or a print out of this activity to add at the end. Educator points to icon or card that was sent home for individual POP Charts.]. *That way, we can practice Write and Rip whenever our emotions feel heavy or hard. This activity is a positive way to manage our emotions, and is also an easy thing to do if we are at home and need a break. Given all of the heavy emotions that have filled us during this time of remote learning, this activity can be used frequently to help us deal with our emotions.*

To begin, pause for a moment and close your eyes. Or, if closing your eyes doesn't feel ok today, pick something to focus on, like a book in the bookcase. Let's all take a few deep breaths together [educator models]. Is there anything that is making you anxious or worried today?

We're going to practice Write and Rip by writing our worries on a piece of paper, then ripping it up and tossing it into the recycle bin or trash can at home. I am going to set the time for two minutes. When the two minutes are over, we will all rip up our papers and toss our worries into the recycling bin. [Educator demonstrates using trash bin in her remote setting appropriately.] *Tossing our worries into the recycling bin helps us work through unpleasant emotions and be ready to learn. No one will see what you write, even me. All our papers are ripped up and placed in the recycling bin or trash can.*

Figure 3.1 Writing on a Piece of Paper.

Once we have finished ripping up our papers, and we place them in the recycle or trash can, these thoughts and feelings are also "thrown away."

Before we begin, I need a student who can restate the activity in their own words.

[Educator calls on student demonstrating the expectations. Student restates activity.]

Thank you, [student name]. Room [x], do we see any potential problems with implementing this activity? [Educator calls on one or two students to discuss potential pitfalls.]

Thank you, [student names]. So, now that we know where the problems may occur, what Agreements do we need to make for the activity to feel safe and accessible for all of us? What are the consequences if the Agreements are broken?

> ★ **Educator Tip:** For this consensus-building strategy to be successful, it is imperative that you consistently uphold the Agreements and carry out the consequences, if the Agreements are broken.

We have time for three students to share their thoughts. Before we share, let's remember to listen intently to others and be careful not to interrupt our classmates.

[Educator calls on students and writes or posts the Agreements and consequences. This is also the perfect time for the educator to suggest modifications to ensure everyone feels included, comfortable, and able to participate.]

Thank you, Room [x], for sharing your thoughts respectfully and thoughtfully. I witnessed students actively listening to their peers. Well done! Now, please get out your pencils and a piece of scratch paper. Once the activity is complete, in your setting, place the recycle or trash bin somewhere near you, so you know that it is "safe" from others in your household. When I say "Begin" I will turn on the music. You will have two minutes to write or draw any negative emotions or worries you may have. When the song is over, we will all rip up our papers and toss them in the recycle bin or trash can.

★ **Tip for Early Childhood or Special Education Teachers:** This activity can be done as a "Draw and Rip" in the same way that older students write their worries, students in early childhood or with other developmental delays can draw and rip, or select pictures printed or in magazines to rip. This builds students' awareness of what causes negative and distracting emotions and provides them with a positive and productive way to alleviate these feelings and focus on tasks at hand in any age range.

Focused Breath

✓ Educator Script

Supplies:

◆ Sentence strip or icon to add the activity to the POP Chart

Time: 3 minutes

The Why Behind the Activity: *Today, we are practicing* **Focused Breath**. *We can practice Focused Breath in class, during synchronous, anytime we need a minute to pause, regulate and focus on our breathing. Focused Breath is wonderful to use when we are feeling overwhelmed or upset, or any time we feel scattered.*

I have already created an icon for Focused Breath and added it to our virtual POP Chart [educator points to icon—if utilizing individual POP Charts, be sure all students have an icon to add]. *That way, we can practice it whenever we like. This activity is a positive way to manage our emotions, and is also an easy thing to do if we are at home and need a break.*

First: *If you feel comfortable, close your eyes or focus your gaze on one point that is not moving. Focus on your breath. Follow your breath as it moves in and out. Try not to change the speed or rhythm of your breath. Leave it just as it is. As you continue to breathe, notice if you feel anything in your body. There is no right or wrong way. Just breathe.*

Then: *Listen for a sound far away. Choose one sound outside of your workspace to focus on. Focus all of your attention on that sound. Breathe it in, and breathe it out for the next ten breaths.* [Educator softly counts to 10.]

Next: *Leave that noise behind and focus your attention on a sound that is closer to you, such as a noise inside your workspace like the hum of a computer or the buzz of an overhead light. Listen only to one sound, nothing else. Breathe it in, and breathe it out for the next ten breaths.* [Educator softly counts to 10.]

Last: *Leave both sounds behind and focus only on the soft, quiet sound of your own breathing. For the next ten breaths observe only the sound of your breathing, tune out everything else.* [Educator softly counts to 10.]

Now clear your mind. Before you open your eyes or return your focus to our virtual space, check in with how you are feeling. Has your breath changed? What do you need to do to

be focused in this present moment? What actions do you need to take? Before we move on, repeat this statement three times in your mind, "I give myself permission not to be perfect. The most important thing is that I try my best." [Educator repeats the statement softly three times.]

Finally, as we close our Focused Breath today, picture yourself being centered, relaxed, and present.

If your eyes are closed, open them. Identify three items that look familiar, such as a chair, a pencil, or a book. Remember, you can practice Focused Breath in class when you experience an emotional distraction to recenter yourself, or during asynchronous time when you are distracted or otherwise disconnected from the classroom or class work.

Memory Minute

Supplies:

- ◆ Index card or icon to add the activity to the POP Chart
- ◆ Timer

Time: 3 minutes

The Why Behind the Activity: *Today, we are practicing Memory Minute. We can practice Memory Minute in class or at home, anytime we need a break. Breaks are healthy for our minds and help us relax. Especially during remote learning, we have a tendency to spend too much time working, which can lead to frustration or other unhealthy emotions. Taking these short and focused breaks will enable increased regulation during work times.*

First: Make sure your room is quiet and that all screens are turned off. Have students turn off their cameras, but ensure they can still hear and have their microphones on. Tell students you are holding up a blank, white piece of paper. Ask the students to close their eyes, if they feel comfortable (remembering to offer the trauma-informed choice to leave the eyes open), and visualize the white sheet of paper in their minds.

Then: Set the timer for 60 seconds and ask the students to remain quiet, which may remind them to breathe quietly, so it is audible only to themselves. Ask the students to keep their voices and bodies quiet, thinking only of the white sheet of paper. For 60 seconds everyone, including the adults in the room, are quiet and focused. No screens, no distractions. (Let's remember, this is an important well-being break for the educators as well!)

Next: When the 60 seconds has concluded, gently cue the students to open their eyes, turn on their cameras, and to bring their focus back to the speaker.

Figure 3.2 A Student Thinking of What to Write.

Last: To cultivate student Self-Awareness, engage your class in a discussion of how this activity felt. Do they feel relaxed and calm after the practice? Was 30 seconds too long/ short? How do their bodies feel after the activity?

★ **Educator Tip:** Once the students have practiced the activity for a few weeks, feel free to increase the time by 15 second intervals.

Equal Breath

✓ Educator Script

Supplies:

◆ Index card or icon to add the activity to the POP Chart

Time: 3 minutes

The Why Behind the Activity: Today, we are practicing Equal Breath. We can practice Equal Breath when we are feeling worried or scared. This activity is a positive way to regulate our emotions anytime we need a break in class or at home.

I have already created an icon/card for Equal Breath and added it to our POP Chart [educator points to card/icon].

First: *Begin seated and place your feet flat on the floor, roll your shoulders back and lengthen your spine.*

Then: *Notice the pattern of your breath. Pay attention to the rhythm and flow of the inhalations and the exhalations. Which is longer? Which is deeper?*

Next: *With your next breath, make your inhalation and exhalation the same length. Let's start with the count of 4. Slowly count to 4 as you inhale.* [Educator slowly counts aloud.] *1-2-3-4. Now, also count to 4 as you exhale. The exercise is to match the length of your breath in, or inhalation, and with your breath out, or exhalation. Breathe in for the count of 4.* [Educator slowly counts aloud.] *1-2-3-4. Breathe out for the count of 4.* [Educator slowly counts aloud.] *1-2-3-4.*

Figure 3.3 A Student Counting Their Breath.

Last: *Let's extend the exhalation to the count of 5. Breathing in for the count of 4 and breathing out for the count of 5. Making the exhalation longer than the inhalation has a calming effect on the nervous system. Please take five more breaths, extending the exhalation longer than the inhalation. If you have asthma you may wish to shorten your breaths, and that is okay too. Practice however it feels comfortable for you, in your body!*

★ **Educator Tip:** Visibly count along on your fingers to help students keep the pace of the activity.

4

School Connectedness and Teacher Trust

Now that you have some tools to help students develop Self-Awareness and practice Self-Regulation, we will move on to the important notion that the development of high quality, caring relationships with educators is critical to all student learning. The development of relationships is made significantly more difficult during periods of remote learning due to the lack of proximity. For all students, teacher feedback in a high trust environment must be integrated into the learning cycle. In this chapter, we will focus on activities that help students of all ages increase their connectedness to school and the classroom, and help build and develop the relationships between students and teachers and enable teacher trust.

School connection is the belief by students that adults in the school care about their learning and about them as individuals. Students are more likely to succeed when they feel connected to school. Critical requirements for feeling connected include high academic rigor and expectations coupled with support for learning, positive adult–student relationships, and physical and emotional safety. Connection to school not only takes time and deep and consistent work, but building relational trust, developing a positive identity, and feeling like you "belong" at school is made even more challenging when in a virtual setting.

DOI: 10.4324/9781003183204-5

School Connectedness and Teacher Trust in Early Childhood and Elementary School

Establishing a connection to school for students in early childhood and elementary school is especially challenging when students have never physically been in the classroom, or experienced the school community. Early childhood students can be highly visual learners, and the lack of physical and visual interaction with their surroundings due to virtual learning, can impact their connection to school and their trust, or lack thereof, with their teachers. It is critical that educators really consider students learning styles and developmental levels in order to ensure they are able to set up a classroom community that meets students needs.

Working to establish school connectedness and teacher trust in a remote setting involves both whole group and individual activities and approaches to student connection. In the following text you will find a few activities that can help further trust building and connectedness in a remote setting. We encourage readers who want to find additional ways to increase school connectedness and teacher trust specifically in a remote setting where students have school provided devices at home to visit www.ClassCatalyst.com to learn more about *Class Catalyst* and *Five to Thrive*, our SEL EdTech platforms that provide quick, natural ways to begin or end any period, or to ensure that students are regularly connecting with teachers even when they are learning asynchronously.

Compliment Partners

Time: 7 minutes

Supplies:

- ◆ Icon to add the activity to the POP Chart
- ◆ Music

The Why Behind the Activity: Today, we are practicing **Compliment Partners** to help us manage vulnerability and develop our **active listening and community-building skills**. This activity also helps us stay healthy by giving us an opportunity to get up and out of our seats.

First: Play music and ask your students to turn on their cameras and dance around in their space at home. They can choose to be on or off camera to dance, but should return to the camera when the music is turned off.

Then: The educator announces which student in the pair will go first (birthday closest to today, bigger/smaller shoe size, etc.). The teacher will split the students into breakout rooms and the person who goes first (birthday closest to today, etc.) will compliment his/her partner by witnessing a time that the other student was exhibiting a positive SEL social behavior such as being kind, compassionate, caring, a team player, a good listener, or thinking about solutions instead of problems.

Next: Give each partner 45 seconds to share a compliment. Close the breakout rooms and have all students return to the main room. Put the music on and continue the activity for three more rounds, ensuring that the teacher recreates breakout rooms each time to ensure partners are changed.

Last: To close the activity, ask the students to return to the main room. The teacher can either use the whiteboard feature on google meet or insert a jamboard in the chat for students to go to. Each student should write "I am _____" on the board. Cue the students to turn one compliment that they received into an "I am" statement such as "I am kind," or "I am a good listener." To close the activity, the students will practice a mini-meditation. For one minute, they will breathe in and breathe out their "I am" statement, as if it were on a continuous loop in their minds. Once the students have their "I am" statements, invite them to sit up tall, shoulders rolled back, and eyes closed, and set the timer for one minute.

★ **Educator Tip:** For the compliment sharing component of this activity to be successful, it is important you appropriately frame the activity by discussing the difference between a true, observational compliment and a joke or self-deprecating comment. A true compliment might be, "You are a very thoughtful and punctual person because you are always on time when we get on our morning meeting," instead of, "I like that you are on time more now because you used to be lazy and show up late, and that was really annoying because I hated waiting for you."

Tap Our Worries Away

Supplies:

◆ Icon to add the activity to the POP Chart

Time: 5 minutes

The Why Behind the Activity: *Today, we are practicing Tap Our Worries Away. We can practice Tap Our Worries Away at home during or outside of school, anytime we are feeling worried or nervous.*

Step One: Make sure your room is quiet. Students may turn off their cameras or choose to leave them on for the activity. The key is to ensure students are not a distraction to others.

Step Two: To demonstrate *Tap Your Worries Away* for the students, make two fists and hold them up in front of your chest. Now, raise your pointer fingers to make the number 1. Bring them together to touch (like a little triangle). Cue the students to do the same.

Step Three: Ask the students to take a few deep breaths and picture something that is making them nervous or worried.

Step Four: Ask the students to tap their index fingers together as you softly say in unison "Tap, tap, tap. Tap, tap, tap. Tap your worries away." (Repeat three times.) When the practice has concluded, gently cue the students to lower their hands and notice how they are feeling.

Step Five: To cultivate student Self-Awareness, engage your class in a discussion of how this activity felt. Do they feel relaxed and calm after the practice? Do they feel less worried or nervous? How could they practice this activity at home or anytime they were feeling worried?

Color Breath

✓ **Educator Script**

Time: 5 minutes

Supplies:

◆ Icon to add the activity to the POP Chart

The Why Behind the Activity: *Today, we are practicing Color Breath to help us learn about how the breath moves in and out of our bodies. Color Breath builds our body awareness by teaching us about our breathing. This activity also gives us an opportunity to learn about our classmates and their favorite colors.*

First: *Sit up tall and proud in your seat.*

Then: *I will choose a student who has demonstrated our Classroom Rules today to pick their favorite color.* [Select a student, and have them share their favorite color.]

Next: *Let's all take a deep breath and close our eyes.*

Last: *Exhaling together, let's chant the color chosen. (For example: "Grrreeeeeeeeeeeennn.")* [Teacher and aides model, assisting students that need help. Please note: multisyllabic words will need to be modelled for the class ahead of time. For instance, lavender becomes Llllllaaaaaa-veeeeennnn-ddddeeeerrr. Or, encourage students to choose monosyllabic colors like red, green, blue, gold, white, black, grey, pink, tan, teal or brown.]

School Connectedness and Teacher Trust in Middle School and High School

By the time they are in high school, as many as 40 to 60 percent of all students—urban, suburban, and rural—are chronically disengaged from school (Blum, 2005). Many recent studies reinforce this notion, and assert that this trend has been accelerated by the pandemic and the increased presence of remote learning. Since March 2020, an estimated three million historically marginalized students have not received any formal education—either they have dropped out or do not formally attend remote learning opportunities offered by their schools (Korman, O'Keefe, & Repka, 2020). This is even more dire in the high school and middle school ages.

Working to establish school connectedness and teacher trust in a remote setting involves both whole group and individual activities and approaches to student connection. In the following text you will find a few activities that can help further this trust building and connectedness in a remote setting as a class group. We encourage readers who want to find additional ways to increase school connectedness and teacher trust specifically in a remote setting where students have school provided devices at home to visit www. ClassCatalyst.com to learn more about Class Catalyst and Five to Thrive, our SEL EdTech platforms that provide quick, natural ways to begin or end any period, or to ensure that students are regularly connecting with teachers even when they are learning asynchronously.

Holding Who I Am

Supplies:

- ◆ Icon to add the activity to the POP Chart
- ◆ Notebook or scratch paper
- ◆ Pens and pencils
- ◆ Clock or timer

Time: 5 minutes

The Why Behind the Activity: Today, we are practicing Holding Who I Am. This activity helps us understand ourselves by identifying, naming, and accepting our strengths and our challenges. The activity helps us learn to be compassionate and kind to ourselves, just as we hope to be compassionate and kind to others.

I have already created an icon for Holding Who I Am and added it to our POP Chart. If you have your own POP Chart at home, please add a card or icon when we are finished.

First: Cue the students to sit up tall, roll their shoulders back, find their feet and take ten deep breaths. [Educator models.] As the students breathe, ask them to reflect on both their strengths and their challenges. Encourage them to be as non-judgmental as possible—operating from a place of being curious instead of critical.

Then: Ask the students to trace one hand on a sheet of paper. Then, cue the students to write or draw all of their strengths inside the hand using "I" statements, such as "I am a good sibling," "I try my best in math," or "I am kind to others."

Next: Around the outside of the hand, ask the students to write the challenges they are working through such as, "I am trying to be less impulsive," "I am working on being kinder to my little brother."

Last: When their papers are complete, cue the students to take five deep breaths to reflect on what they wrote. After their five breaths, ask the students to add a few additional words or phrases to their hands.

★ **Educator Tip:** If time permits, ask the students to share their drawings with a partner by breaking them up into breakout rooms. This is a great way to facilitate peer-to-peer communication and to help students manage vulnerability. Additionally, consider where students may want to store their drawings. The students can keep all their drawings in a notebook, folder, or binder, or they can tape them somewhere visible in their at home learning space.

5

Social Awareness
Activities to Promote Social Interaction Virtually

As students enter and move through the educational journey PK-12th grade, their ability to engage with others effectively becomes more crucial at each step along the spectrum. Therefore, in addition to the development of Self-Awareness and Self-Regulation in settings where students need to implement tools to feel independently successful, finding tools and ways to monitor and regulate, as well as collaborate with others, is an important part of the learning process. This social awareness practice is also made exceptionally more difficult when students are learning in a hybrid or remote setting, as the social aspect is changed in a remarkable way. This is because the "traditional" school setting typically provides the opportunity for rich interactions that support learning, increase resilience, and help mitigate the impact of anxiety and stress.

Social awareness is developed through interaction and peer relationships, and distance learning and other social distancing strategies have made the development and operationalization of peer relationships even more challenging than in a typical school year. The activities and recommendations that follow take the Mindful Practices' in-class activities for developing social awareness and modify them for the distance learning setting while still attending to the development of those important peer relationships.

DOI: 10.4324/9781003183204-6

One Word Check-In   EC – HS

✓ Educator Script

Supplies:

- ◆ Icon to add the activity to the POP Chart

Time: 5 minutes

The Why Behind the Activity: *Today, we are practicing* **One Word Check-In** *to continue to develop our leadership and community-building skills. This activity helps us develop an* ***awareness of our classmates and ourselves*** *and cultivate our ability to put voice to our feelings and emotions.*

First: Log on and ensure all students have the class in "gallery view." Ask your class to: *Look around and notice who is in the class with you and appreciate their unique contributions and special talents. Now, take a breath and remember all the unique and special talents that YOU bring to this class as well.*

Then: Find a student that is demonstrating your classroom Agreements to act as Captain for the activity. The activity will begin with a **one word check-in**, which allows you, as the educator, to step in and participate once the directions have been given.

Next: Choose a cue from the following list that is most relevant to your students' lives, demonstrating your investment in the school community and their lives. Beginning with the Captain, ask the class to say one word that describes _____ (see list)

- ◆ who you are
- ◆ what our classroom community means to you
- ◆ what it feels like to be you
- ◆ how you positively contribute to this school
- ◆ something of which you are proud
- ◆ what is unique about you
- ◆ a special talent or interest that you have
- ◆ something challenging you are working through
- ◆ an example of teamwork you have seen in the past week
- ◆ what keeps you from giving up when things get hard
- ◆ how you stay motivated when you fail and don't succeed
- ◆ how you relax and focus when you are anxious
- ◆ something that motivates you

- ◆ how you move from feeling powerless to empowered
- ◆ what being the solution means to you
- ◆ how loss or grief feels to you
- ◆ what student voice means to you
- ◆ what student agency means to you

Last: Once each student has said their word, the teacher leads the class in one communal breath: *Everyone, now that we've checked in using our one word, I'd like you to take a breath with an even five count inhale and exhale while repeating your word to yourself.*

★ **Educator Tip:** You can use any word cloud program to record the words students are saying and create a visual representation of the words felt by each student. This "cloud" can remain as a visual on your class screen for entrance each day, or remain in your learning management system and returned to anytime.

Shoulder Share⋆   EC – HS

✓ **Educator Script**

Supplies:

◆ Icon to add the activity to the POP Chart
◆ Clock or timer

Time: 5 minutes

The Why Behind the Activity: Today, we are practicing Shoulder Share to develop our interpersonal and relationship-building skills, our compassion for self and others, our positive youth identity and managing our vulnerability. This activity also helps us use our voices to step into agency and stay healthy by getting us up and out of our seats to move.

First: Write an SEL prompt on the screen that you would like your students to discuss, such as how to be kind and compassionate with self and others, or ways in which to creatively contribute to your classroom community. Play music and place the students into paired breakout rooms.

Then: Announce via message to all rooms, which student in the pair will go first (birthday closest to today, bigger/smaller shoe size, etc.). That student will be the first speaker to respond to the prompt.

Next: Give each partner one minute to share their thoughts. When the speaker is sharing, the listener does not speak. The listener does not offer an opinion or advice, they simply listen to the speaker. Once the minute concludes, the speaker and listener switch. Before the music begins again and you close the rooms to come back into the main room, ask the students to give each other an acknowledgment (air hug, high five or thumbs up emoji) to show respect for them and what they shared today. Continue the activity for three more rounds, ensuring you mix up the breakout rooms each time.

In the last round, allow an extra 30 seconds for each student to retell their partner's story. This is done without judgement, evaluation, or advice. The job of the *re-teller* is to act as a mirror to help their partner witness their own words. "What I heard you say was . . . "

Last: When the third round has concluded, close all breakout rooms and welcome students back into the main room for class. To close the activity, your students will practice a mini-meditation. For one minute, they will silently breathe in and breathe out a single sentence related to the prompt, such as "When I feel anxious I can _____," or "Owning my feelings sounds like_____," as if it were on a continuous loop in their minds. Set the timer for one minute and invite your students to sit up tall with their shoulders rolled back and their eyes closed or their gaze focused.

★ **Educator Tip:** As a great stress management activity prior to test taking, have your students share a worrisome thought or feeling such as, "I am afraid I am going to fail," or, "I feel like I am going to do a terrible job!" Instruct each partner to respond by asking a follow-up question such as "Can you tell me more?" or "What can you do when you feel anxious or stressed?"

Gratitude Journal   EC – HS

✓ Educator Script

Supplies:

- ◆ Icon to add the activity to the POP Chart
- ◆ 20–25 photos or drawings of people, places, objects, occasions, animals, etc. (Please note: the educator should choose images of diverse cultures, races, lifestyles, and ethnicities. Be intentional and avoid any images that may be triggering or be culturally insensitive.)
- ◆ Notebook or scrap paper
- ◆ Pens and pencils
- ◆ Clock or timer

Time: 10 minutes

The Why Behind the Activity: Today, we will be writing a Gratitude Journal. The practice of being grateful helps us acknowledge and express our emotions, engage in perspective taking and cultivate social awareness. When we build an awareness of how others' actions and demonstrations of appreciation impact us, we become more aware of how our actions and demonstrations of appreciation impact others as well.

First: Display a slideshow of the chosen images. Play the slideshow to the entire group. As the images circulate, ask students: *Do you connect with any one photo more than another? Observe what you are experiencing when you look at the different pictures. Try not to judge your reactions, just notice them.*

Next: Instruct your students: *Now that we have finished viewing the images, you will have four minutes to write or draw something that expresses the gratitude you are feeling. There is no right or wrong way to express your story of gratitude in this moment. You can explain which photo resonated with you and why. You can tell a story from your childhood or from last week. The only requirement is that your pen is in motion for the entire four minutes. Get your pens ready—take a breath—and begin!* [Educator sets the timer for four minutes and writes "Start Time:" and "Stop Time:" on the screen or sets the virtual countdown timer for all to see.]

Last: Stop the timer and cue students to put their pens down. Ask your students to take five breaths and examine what they created. Then ask your students to: *Notice what you are feeling in the body and in the mind. Do you feel any different after your gratitude practice? How could you practice gratitude daily?* [Close the activity with a quick Thumb Check. Or, if time permits, facilitate a Talking Stick discussion.]

6

Student Voice and Agency

Student voice and agency has been well researched and documented as a way to increase school engagement for all students, as well as impact student achievement and success over time. Increasing student voice enables students to have input into their educational choices, which includes their SEL choices and development of SEL competencies. Due to the decentralization of students that occurs as a result of remote learning, and the decreased amount of synchronous learning, educators often find it challenging to increase the level of student voice and agency in the remote learning setting.

DOI: 10.4324/9781003183204-7

Activities for Creating Student Voice and Agency

Goal Setting Postcard   EC – HS

The Why Behind the Activity: *Today, we are practicing **Goal Setting Postcard** to help us be personally responsible and accountable. This activity is great for reminding us that we can be the solution in our own lives when we feel frustrated or are facing a challenging task.*

In-Person:

1. *Create a slide with the following script on it:*

In the next two weeks I will _____ [action verb] at _____ [time/day] because _____ [reason for action]. My colleague_____ [name of staff member] will help me reach my goal, if I need support. One problem I will need to watch out for is_____ [potential problem]. I can be the solution by _____ [action verb]. Signed:_____ Date:_____ Witnessed:_____ Date:_____

2. Ask students to copy the text onto a piece of paper in front of them. Split students up into breakout rooms with pairs or triads for completion and brainstorming together to fill out the blanks.
3. On the back of the paper, ask students to draw a picture of themselves completing their goal, or draw their facial expression when completing the goal.
4. Once their Goal Setting Postcards are complete, ask the students to review what they have written and drawn. Invite them to sit up tall and close their eyes. For one minute, ask the students to visualize what it would look, feel, and sound like to meet their goal. Ask them to visualize themselves reaching their goal. Once the minute concludes, ask for a few students to give you a one word check-in, sharing one word about their goal.

Note for Teacher: Have students screenshot or take a picture of their goal postcard and submit it to you. Wait eight–ten weeks, then mail them to each student's home address.

*Adapted from Kripalu Center for Yoga and Health's *Kripalu Yoga in the Schools Curriculum* (2015).

Community-Based Service Learning Project EC – HS

✓ **Educator Script**

Supplies:

◆ *To be determined based upon project chosen*

Estimated Project Time: *3–4 weeks*

The Why Behind the Activity: *We are planning and participating in a Service Learning Project to connect with and give back to our community. In Social Emotional Learning this year/semester we have worked hard to develop our leadership, collaboration, teamwork, and peer-to-peer communication skills. We have worked on being the solution and on developing our voice and agency of our classroom community. Now, we will create a Service Learning Project to step into action and be the solution for folks in our larger community in or outside of school.*

Service Learning Project: Having students work collaboratively to create a Service Learning Project is the perfect way to reinforce a sense of community. Service Learning Projects are most successful when they bring different groups together, such as one classroom partnering with an older/younger grade to plan a school green space or to read poetry at the local senior center, whether in-person or online.

Prior to the start of the project, it is important to message the concept of responsible giving and/or *giving back* to the community. Instead of framing the Service Learning Project as a one-sided proposition of *us* helping *them*, discuss the ways in which *giving back* to the community creates an opportunity for the class to contemplate their role within the community, to share their voice with community members, to collaborate in the creation of something meaningful and relevant and to engage in a relationship of reciprocal learning. It is also crucial that the students set goals around the project, measure its impact and examine prospects for sustainability, thus moving away from one-off monetary gifts and instead developing positive youth identity by being the solution and giving back via human connection.

> ★ **Educator Tip:** Some states, such as Illinois, have Service Learning Standards that connect nicely to their Social Emotional Learning standards (in this case, most notably, "Goal 3 – Demonstrate decision-making skills and responsible behaviors in personal, school, and community contexts"). Connecting these standards can be a great way to create metrics to measure the overall impact of the project.

Thought Partner Debrief   EC – HS

Supplies:

- ◆ Icon to add the activity to the POP Chart
- ◆ Music

Time: 7 minutes

The Why Behind the Activity: *Today, we are learning **Thought Partner Debrief** to practice sharing our voices in peer-to-peer communication through collaboration and active, attuned listening. Respectful communication, where we are fully present and engaged, is key to positively and compassionately contributing to our classroom community.*

First: Arrange your students into pairs in breakout rooms. Inform your students who will be going first (i.e. longer/shorter hair, birthday closest/furthest from today, etc.).

Then: Give your students a question or prompt via breakout room message. Before they begin sharing, invite your students to sit up tall and close their eyes. Ask your students to take a mindfulness minute by breathing easily and collecting their thoughts.

Next: Ask your students to sit and ensure they are looking at their partners on the screen. The first student shares their thoughts for one minute while the other listens quietly. When the minute is up, the educator will message the rooms to "SWITCH."

Last: After each partner has had a turn, cue your students that they will have [x] amount of time to discuss the topic. When the time is up, the educator can either have the pairs join another pair in a breakout room to share, or return to the whole class session and share out. (Remind students what active listening looks, sounds, and feels like in this activity.)

Conclude the activity with a whole-group **Thumb Check**.

★ **Educator Tip:** This is a great opportunity to work on consensus-building with your students! Depending on the topic, when the time has concluded, your students must be able to report on one point that they both agree on, and one point on which they both have different points of view.

Owning My Story   EC – HS

Supplies: Icon to add the activity to the POP Chart

- ◆ Notebook or scratch paper
- ◆ Pens and pencils
- ◆ Clock or timer

Time: 10 minutes

The Why Behind the Activity: *Today, we will be writing an Owning My Story Journal. The author Brene Brown wrote: "Owning our story and loving ourselves through that process is the bravest thing we will ever do." Writing this journal today will help us practice being compassionate with ourselves and* **bravely accepting our strengths as well as our challenges.** *As we create our stories, it is important to remember that these stories do not define us, they simply help us own the experiences that make us who we are. For instance, if Ruthie fails a test, it does not mean she is a failure. Ruthie's story is what she learned from failing that test. Failing is a step in learning. As Albert Einstein said, "You never fail until you stop trying."*

I have already created an icon for Owning My Story Journal and added it to our virtual POP Chart [educator points to icon]. *If you have your own individual POP Chart at home, please add a card that looks like this* [shows card] *now.*

First: As the students fold their papers in half. On the top half of their papers, ask the students to write the sentence starter below:

Today, I am telling my story of _____.

Then: Read the following words/phrases. Ask the students to complete their sentences with the words/phrases that resonate with them in this moment.

- ◆ Trusting my gut
  Failing
  Being grateful
  Being happy
  Being the solution
  Teamwork
  Losing
- ◆ Being kind and compassionate to myself
  Being kind and compassionate to others

- ◆ Feeling misunderstood
- ◆ Forgiveness
- ◆ Humility
- ◆ Being vulnerable
- ◆ Managing anger
- ◆ Winning gracefully
- ◆ Losing gracefully
- ◆ Keeping my cool in a tough situation
- ◆ Being strong
- ◆ Trying my best
- ◆ Being creative
- ◆ Taking a risk
- ◆ Being fair
- ◆ Following through
- ◆ Being honest
- ◆ Over-sharing
- ◆ Keeping my word
- ◆ Being enough
- ◆ Communicating
- ◆ Finding my voice
- ◆ Listening to my body
- ◆ Letting go
- ◆ Doing the right thing

Next: On the bottom half of their papers, give the students five minutes to write a paragraph, illustrate a drawing, create a cartoon, compose a poem, etc. that tells their story, in their own words.

Last: Once their drafts are complete, cue the students to take five deep breaths [educator models]. At this point, they may choose to make edits or changes to their stories, drawings, or cartoons. If desired, give the students a timeline for completing their creations, or an invitation to work on them at home for extra credit. On the back of their papers, ask the students to write out and sign the following sentence:

I give myself permission not to be perfect. The most important thing I can do each day is try my best. Signed, _____ Date_____

★ **Educator Tip:** If your class has a relationship with a younger grade, facilitating an experience for your students to share their stories is a great way to help them manage vulnerability, engage in community-building, and demonstrate leadership. (What positive modeling for the younger students!) Additionally, think of where you would like your students to store their stories and drawings. The students can keep them all in a notebook, folder, or binder.

Or, perhaps share their stories with parents and caregivers? This can even be done in the virtual classroom by sharing an online space, breaking students up into breakout rooms and ensuring students stay connected not just in their class pods, but throughout the school.

★ **Educator Tip:** This is a great pre-teaching activity for the Community-Based Service Learning Project or for students who need help setting post-secondary goals. Students can complete their Goal-Setting Postcards in teams. This activity can also be used to set goals for your classroom community or to help your students, as a collective, overcome obstacles that are negatively impacting their learning environment.

7

Virtual SEL for Collaborative Planning with Colleagues

Collaboration is always an important element amongst teachers in a school, but it has become even more challenging with the onset of the remote learning environment. This is because teachers are now required to teach both synchronously and asynchronously and have various other responsibilities for connecting with students and families, and in their own homes, as well. Therefore, ensuring that as teachers and leaders in the remote environment, we are all working collaboratively is critical, albeit exceptionally challenging.

As the famous African proverb states, "If you want to go fast, go alone. If you want to go far, go together." In order to facilitate collaborative and collegial planning and staff meetings, we have adapted many of our student activities to meet the needs of the virtual environment for staff. As educators, we well know that Self-Awareness and Self-Regulation as well as social awareness are critical elements not only for our students to continually practice, but for us educators to do the same. Therefore, we have added this chapter to help teachers and leaders pause, own it, and practice using tools aligned specifically to the tools your students are practicing to continually develop socio-emotional competence. These can be used in grade level team meetings, as teachers or leaders lead professional development in the whole staff setting, or anytime you are working with a colleague or need some time for self-care.

DOI: 10.4324/9781003183204-8

Spider Web Connecting and Owning My Own Story

The Why: All humans are social beings, and connections are critical. When new people join the community or a new community is coming together (beginning of the school year as an example), it is important to facilitate finding peer connections for adults, just as it is critical for students.

In-Person
If your staff is in-person, you can do this activity at a safe social distance.

1. Create a circle (or with more than 12 people, multiple non-intersecting circles). Each person should be 6 ft. from the next person.
2. One person starts with a large ball of yarn (as a fun addition, we use our school colors).
3. The person states their name, role, number of years at the school, why they chose to join this school community in particular and then connects to someone else in the circle by throwing the yarn ball to them (keeping one end with them) and stating the connection. Since it is the first day with staff, some know each other well, and can connect on many personal attributes but some have to connect on their names, physical attributes, wearing the same shoes, and other things!
4. Repeat Step #3 until all members of the circle have a small piece of yarn connected to the rest of the web.
5. Look at the web. It is amazing to notice all of the connections that ALREADY exist.
6. Commit to making more connections (or at least one new connection) before next week's meeting.
7. Cut a portion of the yarn. Create a piece of jewelry (necklace, bracelet, anklet, bookmark, headband, etc.) from the piece you've cut to remind you of your connection to this amazing staff throughout next week!
8. Use a notecard each week to write down WHO and WHEN you will connect with one new colleague.

Virtual
1. Open Jamboard (part of the google suite—it's free!).
2. Share with your school team.
3. Use the circle tool and draw a large circle.
4. Ask each staff member to insert their bitmoji, picture, representative meme or formal school picture) as if they were standing as part of the circle.

5.   In your meeting, select the person to start, and have him/her use the pen tool to "throw the yarn" to a colleague and connect (see Step #3 above for in-person meetings).

6.   Follow the preceding Steps #4–8. Since you can't cut a piece of virtual yarn, you can send cheap rubber bracelets to all or just have people share their notecards for accountability!

Activity: Holistic Self-Care Wheel Assessment

The Self-Care Wheel has been adapted from Mary Jo Barrett, MSW and can be used with students and staff alike.

The Why: In spite of wishful thinking, humans have a limited supply of energetic resources. Assessing both the energy expenditures and replenishers in the holistic areas of well-being allows one to prioritize needs for optimal well-being to live a balanced life.

In-Person

1.   Provide a template of the Self-Care Wheel (included earlier in Chapter 2), and make sure it is double sided, with a wheel on each side.

2.   In the wheel, create a list of energy expenditures for each category on the wheel. For example, on the list for "physical," a new mom might indicate middle of the night wakings for the baby as an energy expenditure.

3.   On the back side, use a different color ink and create a list of energy replenishers for each category on the wheel. For example, on the list for "relational," someone might indicate a weekly group that meets around a hobby.

4.   Look at both sides to determine which areas have the fewest replenishers and the most expenditures. These will be your priorities on which to focus for a self-care plan.

Virtual

1.   Send via email the Self-Care Wheel, and ensure participants print two copies of the wheel.

2.   Label one side "Expenditures" and the other side "Replenishers."

3.   Follow the preceding Steps #2–4 using a visual timer on the screen for participants.

Activity: Compassion Fatigue

The Why: Compassion fatigue is the cumulative effect of stress resulting from caring for and helping traumatized or suffering people. Teaching during the time of COVID has certainly led to a variety of issues that relate to teachers and leaders being on a spectrum of toxic stress which can adversely impact your functioning in daily life, and in your job.

This activity is meant to build awareness of the symptoms that you are experiencing which can indicate compassion fatigue. Once awareness is built, coping strategies can be matched to the symptoms.

In-Person
1. Distribute the list of symptoms adults may experience which indicate compassion fatigue.
2. Provide a space and time (staff meeting, team meeting or other joint time) to put on soothing music and provide at least 15 uninterrupted minutes for teacher quiet reflection using the checklist.
3. Use post-it chart paper, and have a different sheet for each of the symptoms (or you can have a four-square on each chart with one symptom in each square.
4. Distribute small dot stickers (any color) to each participant.
5. Participants use dots to indicate where they have placed an x under often.
6. As a group, identify the most common symptoms we have as a group, and compare individually with your own chart.

Virtual
1. Distribute the list of symptoms adults may experience which indicate compassion fatigue (send it via email or ask people to download from a shared drive).
2. Provide a space and time (staff meeting, team meeting or other joint time) to put on soothing music and provide at least 15 uninterrupted minutes for teacher quiet reflection using the checklist.
3. Use ideaboardz.com or Google Jamboard for people to "mark" which symptoms they are most often experiencing.
4. Allow for discussion via zoom during a meeting around these symptoms. School leaders should take note of symptoms most often experienced to help groups and individuals connect with strategies for stress management.

Table 7.1: Compassion Fatigue

Are you experiencing . . .	Rarely	Sometimes	Often
Anger/cynicism			
Fear			
Guilt			
Hopelessness			
Anxiety			
Exhaustion			
Sense of hopelessness			
Living in a state of hypervigilance			
Feeling unsafe/anticipating danger			
Difficulty embracing complexity/tendency toward concrete thinking			
Difficulty listening			
Loss of creativity			
Poor self-care			
Sleeping/eating disturbances			
Increased illness			
Reduced productivity			
Difficulty focusing			
Withdrawal from social activities			
Increased substance use			
A loss of connection and trust in your systems of meaning			
Denial			

Activity: Body Scan

The Why: This activity builds a Self-Awareness practice by inviting you to be in the present moment and sense and feel your body, so you can respond effectively to its needs and care for yourself.

In-Person

1. Begin by detaching from your outer world and shifting your awareness to your body. We invite you to listen to your body.
2. If it is comfortable for you, perhaps you might close your eyes or lower your gaze to an unmoving point in the room.
3. Begin to notice any areas of tension in your body. Notice any areas that feel relaxed. Without any need to do anything with these feelings, simply notice them.
4. Now bring awareness to your body seated wherever you're seated by feeling the weight of your body on the chair or on the floor.
5. Notice the air coming into your body and leaving it.
6. Invite awareness of your feet on the floor. Notice any sensations in the toes, the arch of your feet and your heels. Are your feet heavy? Is there pressure or temperature that you notice?
7. When you are ready, bring your awareness now to your legs against the chair or floor. Notice where you might feel heaviness or pressure. Notice where you might notice lightness.
8. Bring awareness to your back against the chair, scan from the top of the spine to the base focusing on any areas of tension you notice. Then sift to notice where there is no tension in your back.
9. Bring your attention to your stomach area. If it is tense or tight, let it soften. Take a breath as you feel ready.
10. Notice your hands, can you feel tension or tightness? Allow them to soften.
11. Bring awareness to your arms. Do you notice sensations? Notice higher in your shoulders, if they are tense, let them relax.
12. Notice your neck and throat. Bring awareness to any areas of tension or the absence of tension.
13. Focus on your jaw—is it tight or soft? Is your tongue at the roof of your mouth? If so, allow it to drop away.
14. Notice your face and facial muscles. With a breath, allow those muscles in your face and jaw to soften.
15. Now notice your whole body present here in this moment. Be aware of your whole body as much as possible. Breathe Deeply.

16. When you are ready, you can open your eyes and gently come back to the room by noticing and labeling three items you see in the space (in your mind).
17. Reflect on how you feel now.

Virtual

1. Ensure everyone is muted, and that soothing music is playing to help focus if there are distractions in the individual settings.
2. Let participants know that they can leave their video off or on, but that full engagement is critical to the scan working.
3. Begin at #1 in the in-person instructions and go to the end.
4. At #17, ensure everyone's cameras are back on.

8

Engaging Families in the Virtual Environment

For decades it has been said that parents are a child's first teacher. As Maya Angelou once said, *"I became the kind of parent my mother was to me"* (Lupton, 1990). This mantra has never been more true than when students are learning in a virtual environment at home. Dr. Joyce Epstein of Johns Hopkins University (Epstein & Sanders, 2002) developed a framework for defining six different types of parent involvement. This framework assists educators in developing school and family partnership programs. The six keys as described by Epstein apply to family engagement, even in a virtual setting. In the following pages, we will discuss the keys briefly (Parenting, Communicating, Volunteering, Learning at Home, Decision-Making, and Collaborating with the Community) and provide some hands-on connections to SEL that schools can make to keep families engaged in a virtual setting.

Parenting

Schools, teachers, and administrators can work to help families establish home environments that support children as students. This is especially crucial during periods of short- or long-term virtual learning. One way for schools to help families do this is to share the opportunity to create a POP Chart for each student (and even each adult) in a household. The Thumb Check would be another quick way families can engage with their children. This helps everyone use a common language around pausing, owning feelings/thoughts and

DOI: 10.4324/9781003183204-9

behavior, and practicing a tool for regulation. Holding a virtual training session for parents on creating the POP Chart and Thumb Check daily is a wonderful opportunity and we have created the following sample script.

Thumb Check

At any point throughout the day, a parent may ask students for a quick *Thumb Check*. The purpose of a Thumb Check is first and foremost to connect interpersonal relationships between children and adults by the consistent practice of sharing feelings. It is also a practical tool to gauge kids' energy or emotions. The parent simply signals the students to hold their thumbs against their chests, which is quick and easy if the parent is on a work phone call, tending to another child or otherwise engaged in multiple tasks at once.

> Thumbs-Up = I'm experiencing pleasant feelings: calm, relaxed, happy
> Thumbs to the Side = Meh. I'm bored, restless, distracted
> Thumbs-Down = I'm experiencing unpleasant feelings: sad, mad, stressed, hungry

Giving children multiple methods to check in (whether it is via POP Chart or Thumb Check) demonstrates that you are invested in providing opportunities for all your children to practice naming, identifying, and proactively acknowledging their emotions. This is critical for parents as well, especially as students navigate the home-school classroom.

Additionally, encourage all home stakeholders, babysitters, other children, or both parents to check in with children as part of the morning routine and at any point over the course of the remote school day, or a weekend day with a quick Thumb Check. The Thumb Check allows students to use a familiar tool in the home, and the home classroom, and continually develop their regulation skills as their different environments merge in a virtual learning setting.

Starting the Virtual Day with a POP Check

Creating a POP Check at home can be done simply by using tape or tacks on a door, wall or other space that is mutually agreed to by parents and students. If families have multiple siblings, a POP Chart can be created in a shared space—like a kitchen or family room. In our house, we have a POP Chart posted on the sliding door that leads outside from the kitchen. If you do create a POP Chart in a shared space, provide each child with a magnet or paper with double stick tape on the back with their name or picture. As part of the morning routine—during breakfast for us—children move their names to the appropriate place on the chart: Thumbs-Up, Thumbs to the Side, or Thumbs-Down. Children **PAUSE** to check in with how they are feeling. Then, they **OWN IT** by moving their names to indicate their emotions or feelings. Lastly, they choose an activity to **PRACTICE** that will help them be present for the day ahead. When my children have completed their POP Check, they sit down at the table for breakfast.

> **Pause:** Stop for a moment and take a deep breath. What are you thinking? What are you feeling in your body?
>
> **Own It:** Name your emotions and feelings, "I am Happy," "I am Sad," etc.
>
> **Practice:** Find the breathing or movement activity that can help you calm down, focus, and be ready to learn.

For those individual children that have moved their names to indicate they are having a difficult day, find a time during the morning (or whenever they indicate they are challenged) to connect and offer a SEL or mindfulness practice that would meet their needs. Sometimes, they just might need to connect with an adult.

Beyond using a POP Chart or Thumb Check, a virtual learning environment offers a perfect opportunity to engage parents in parent education—including education on SEL, developmental milestones that impact emotional development, and how to solve problems in the home environment. Assisting the families can also occur through utilizing virtual home visits during transition points between elementary, middle, and high schools when in-person home visits may not be possible.

Communicating

Communication with families takes on a new challenge during periods of remote learning, but this type of learning also opens new opportunities for schools, leaders, and teachers. Designing effective forms of school-to-home and home-to-school communication about learning and student progress can be especially challenging in this setting. Integrating the sharing of student socio-emotional learning competencies should also be a part of regular communication with families, especially in the virtual or remote setting.

The following are some questions to guide your school leadership team through when considering how complete your communication is with families, specifically in relation to social emotional learning and student well-being:

- How often do I ask families what is going on at home that could impact (positively or negatively) student interaction in class?
- What feedback do I provide to families on student dispositions in the areas of Self-Awareness, Self-Regulation, social awareness, and responsible decision-making?
- How do I help families set goals for their children in the areas of SEL, alongside the goals they have for academic growth and achievement?
- How do families know the engagement and other SEL expectations of my classroom, in addition to the academic needs of the students?
- Do families communicate their needs with me? Why or why not? How could we facilitate additional two-way communication that benefits all?

Volunteering

Recruiting and organizing parents to help and support the classroom and school community is another area that although at first glance is made more difficult during remote learning, can actually be an opportunity for more families to become engaged in the school community. However, this has not been the case in many settings, as the focus has been placed on physical volunteering and physical safety. With a simple lens shift, schools—including teachers and leaders—can create opportunities for families to become more engaged in the classroom communities and school communities, which overall, can lead to a healthier school community.

Since home becomes the school during days, weeks, months, or years of remote learning, teachers and leaders can ask themselves the following questions when considering the all-important role of volunteering for families in the remote learning environment:

- What opportunities can I provide for family members to be active members of my classroom or school community (rather than just a nosy observer)?
- In what ways can involving family members through volunteering enrich our community and add value for students?
- Do our volunteer opportunities respect the diverse schedules and needs of our families?

Learning at Home

As stated earlier, during virtual learning, the home and school environments become one. Therefore, ensuring parents have information and ideas about how to help students at home with homework and other curriculum-related activities, decisions, and planning is critical. Families also need to understand the developmental growth expectations by grade level in all subject areas, including social emotional learning and growth. This can be in the form of a whole child report card, where different behavioral socio-emotional learning characteristics are discussed through strengths identified and future areas of growth.

Many times, we have personally observed a "no homework" guideline during remote learning. While this is not necessarily the recommended practice, being very diligent as a teacher or leader in determining WHAT and HOW children will bring their learning into their home environment and how we can utilize parents in this process is critical to ensuring that learning at home is a valued proposition in all schools. Key questions for consideration include:

◆ How do students share learning they've engaged in at home with the school's community?
◆ What structures and systems are in place for students to share school learning at home, and to build on it at home?
◆ What skills and characteristics exist in the home environment that we can encourage and build on in the classroom setting?

Decision-making and Collaborating with the Community

In the virtual classroom, it is difficult to include all stakeholders as decision makers and leaders. It is also challenging to find ways to connect families and students to community resources, since many of those environments could also be impacted and services could be converted to a virtual setting as well. Questions to consider for teachers and leaders include the following:

◆ How do we conduct meetings and do we invite families to this setting?
◆ How can families be engaged in decisions that impact their children at the classroom and school level?
◆ Do we know what resources would be helpful for students and

      families to access in our school and in our wider community? How
      do we or can we facilitate this access?
◆   What do we know about student interests and family interests? How
      do we facilitate growth and connection in those areas through the
      school or classroom?

Growing and encouraging the development of social and emotional learning
in children and competencies in adults is critical for overall school success
and engaging families in this process is a key part of the process.

A Candid Note to School Leaders

SEL and mindfulness can often mistakenly be seen as a separate add-on that
requires little or no integration or proficiency on the part of the educator
delivering the remote instruction. Being able to guide students to understand their feelings and emotions in a trauma-informed way requires educators to deeply examine their implicit biases and engage in continual race
and identity development work, which can seem insurmountable, especially
in the virtual classroom. Without culturally responsive integration or practitioner competency, the benefits of SEL can be limited and short term, at best.
SEL and mindfulness are best implemented when they are integrated into
the climate and culture not just of the classroom, but of the larger school and
district.

    In many schools, stakeholders are utilizing effective SEL tools across the
building, but nothing has been codified. While there may be wonderful SEL
and mindfulness practices taking place, there is no common language and
students spend the bulk of their time engaging in a form of SEL code-switching
from room to room, instead of being present in their practice. While these
stakeholders are well intentioned and, most likely, implementing solid practices, the students spend their time decoding what is happening in which setting instead of embodying the practices themselves. This is why high-quality
professional learning opportunities are so important: they create common
language, alignment, and practices across the school building. But, they must
be coupled with clear messaging and expectations from you as to why we
are doing this work and who is expected to do what, especially in the virtual
school setting.

    Most importantly, be very clear about how much time should be devoted
to SEL during remote learning. Do not talk vaguely about priorities. Give
specific amounts of time you expect adults in your building to devote to both
non-instructional SEL skill-building (intentional, interpersonal relationships

between adults and students) and instructional SEL skill-building (teaching SE competencies, embedding SEL into academic content, etc.) each day. Draw a line in the sand, stick to it, and evaluate folks on whether or not they do it. Then, provide every caring adult in your building the training they need to be successful. Remember, training in SEL is not the same as training in how to implement a SEL program. The former trains teachers in SEL as a discipline, the latter trains teachers in how to implement the lessons that come with the kit you purchased. These are not the same thing, especially as most SEL kits are designed for in-person instruction.

Invite all educators in your school building (paraprofessionals, non-certified staff, etc.) to participate in well-being workshops and SEL trainings. Every adult matters because they are part of our community *and* because they all teach students how to be in the world. Don't merely give educators permission for well-being ("No longer is the culture of this school one that rewards self-sacrifice . . . "), be clear about the *times* during their work day when you are giving them space to practice well-being ("The first 20 minutes of our monthly PLC time will be devoted to . . . ") and *when* they are to prioritize SEL over academics ("Non-instructional check-ins should happen each morning for about three minutes and SEL should be embedded into instructional content for an additional ten minutes each day.") Also, let folks know what the expected outcomes will be for their SEL work ("Our projected outcomes are that at least 85 percent of our students will report that they have a caring relationship with at least one adult in . . . "), *who* is expected to practice SEL ("SEL is the job of every caring adult in our school who teaches students how to be in the world . . . ") and, finally, if this work will be part of their formal evaluation.

Should you survey stakeholders for their input before you speak your expectations? Absolutely! But, who do we need to listen to with the most attention? Our students! We need to listen to the voices (all the voices, not just a few kids on the honor roll who are going to tell us what we want to hear) of the students we support! Do not delegate this work to a committee of adults who will spend six months creating Google Docs that will make recommendations that ultimately only have weight if they come from you, and are wholly absent of student voice. Your job is to give everyone—adults and students alike—the road map and boundaries in which to do the work. That includes how time will be prioritized and spent. Folks will only feel comfortable spending time on well-being and SEL if they know you will stand by them when that parent phone call comes in complaining about "instructional minutes lost" and they know that their hard work is something that will reflect favorably on their next evaluation, especially if they are navigating the stressors of remote learning.

Teacher Well-Being: A Lesson for School Administrators on Sources of Stress

It is well-known that teaching is classified as a high-stress career and research over the past several decades supports this (Adams, 2001; Arikewuyo, 2004; Kyriacou, 2001; Milstein & Golaszewski, 1985; Stoeber & Rennert, 2008; Travers & Cooper, 1996; Vandenberghe & Huberman, 1996; Younghusband, Garlie, & Church, 2003). Researchers have found that internal characteristics, such as self-esteem, self-efficacy, and personal behavior, as well as external factors, such as student behavior, workload, work environment, and other colleagues, can contribute to the high level of stress teachers experience on the job (Adams, 2001; Borg, Riding, & Falzon, 1991; Boyle, Borg, Falzon, & Baglioni, 1995; Collie, Shapka, & Perry, 2012; Roeser, Skinner, Beers, & Jennings, 2012). These sources lead to burnout, with such symptoms as emotional exhaustion, anxiety, and a lack of motivation, and commitment (Collie, Shapka, & Perry, 2011; Collie et al., 2012; Roeser et al., 2013). Beyond negative implications for teacher well-being, overly stressed teachers can have negative impacts on student performance, behavior, relationships, and their overall ability to meet student needs (Herman, Hickmon-Rosa, & Reinke, 2018; Reinke, Herman, & Stormont, 2013). Negative experiences from teachers and students alike cumulatively contribute to high turnover rates and toxic school climates (Collie et al., 2011; Howard & Johnson, 2004).

Despite the rising prevalence of teacher education programs and professional development on Social Emotional Learning (SEL), they scarcely prioritize developing skills related to mindfulness, emotional regulation, and coping with stress for teachers and staff (Roeser et al., 2013; Roeser et al., 2012). When schools and districts have implemented programs related to improving social emotional intelligence, they are typically focused on SEL in relation to students and their needs, and less on the SEL impacts and benefits to teachers (Collie et al., 2011; Ransford, Greenberg, Domitrovich, Small, & Jacobson, 2009), though some research proposes that SEL is related to teacher social emotional competence and well-being (Collie et al., 2011; Jennings & Greenberg, 2009).

Existing research suggests that there may be direct and indirect benefits if schools and districts offer mindfulness or SEL training to teachers prior to administering it to students (Roeser et al., 2012; Sarason, 1990). A forthcoming work by Kim, Kakuyama-Villaber, and Gurolnick (2021) further explores the ways in which students and teachers may directly or indirectly affect one another through the lens of stress and well-being. Their research expands upon existing work by shifting the dynamic to center teacher voice and perception and attempt to gain deeper understanding related to experiences of stress (Collie et al., 2012).

The study utilizes the sample of 975 participants in professional development sessions for SEL during the 2018–2019 school year, which is a part of the implementation framework developed by Mindful Practices, where the first phase focuses on teacher support through professional development and the coaching model. Latent Class Analysis (LCA), which identifies unmeasured patterns of class membership using observed variables (Bowers & Sprott, 2012; Duncan, Duncan, & Strycker, 2006; Goodman, 2002; Urick & Bowers, 2014) determined two classes coupled with two subgroups: The first class finds *Students* to be the main source of stress and *Logistics & Environment* to be the subgroup. This class indicates that one source of stress for teachers stems from student behaviors and needs and this leads to a negative and stressful work environment. It is important to distinguish that our category of *Students* includes both stress from negative student behaviors and stress from a teacher's concerns about their inability to meet a student's needs or help them with personal trauma or struggles. This distinction is significant in order to refine the belief that stress from students is exclusively due to disruptive student behavior. The second class identifies *Logistics & Environment* to be the main source of stress with adult dynamics (both *Management* and *Colleagues*) to be the subgroups. This class indicates that stress stemming from the work environment is largely due to an inability to communicate, collaborate, and work with others including supervisors and administration, in addition to colleagues.

While LCA distinguishes two prominent but separate classes or sources of stress, the results also draw attention to the finding of *Logistics & Environment* as an element of both. This supports past findings and our current suggestions that school and district leaders should be allocating time, efforts, and funding to create and maintain a positive school climate that addresses the needs of all people in the building. A last distinction from the findings is that the proportions of the two identified classes indicate that the issues among adults are far more prevalent than those issues from students. These results support the notion that SEL and mindfulness programs should be utilized to improve the well-being of teachers and other school staff, in addition to and potentially even before attending to the social emotional needs of students.

– Anna Gurolnick, Kakuyama-Villaber and Dr. Kiljoong Kim,
Chapin Hall at the University of Chicago

Conclusion

As we continue to navigate the challenges of virtual learning—whether they be intermittent or regular—we continue to believe that prioritizing social emotional learning and the development of social emotional competence in both children and adults is critical to overall success, both in school and in life. For years, schools have mistakenly seen SEL as a quick fix for problem behaviors or a crisis intervention. In the virtual classroom it is essential that we remember SEL is a process, an approach practiced over time. As we look to forge deep and meaningful connections with our students via the digital space we must give students the space to get to know themselves, and give us the time to get to know them. For many of us, human connection is what called us to education. If we take care of our own Social Emotional Competence and well-being, then we can be emotionally available to others and connect with our colleagues and students more authentically.

We hope you are able to use this text in both in-person and virtual learning environments in the future. Continue the conversation by following us at @_coolclassroom or visiting ITeachBecause.com to share your story with educators. We love to engage with our readers and the community of SEL practitioners and thought leaders across the globe.

DOI: 10.4324/9781003183204-10

References

Adams, E. (2001). A proposed causal model of vocational teacher stress. *Journal of Vocational Education and Training, 53*(2), 223–246.

Arikewuyo, M. O. (2004). Stress management strategies of secondary school teachers in Nigeria. *Educational Research, 46,* 195–207.

Bishop, J. B. (1920). *Theodore Roosevelt and his time: Shown in his own letters.*

Blum, R. (2005). *School connectedness: Improving students' lives.* Baltimore, MD: John Hopkins Bloomberg School of Public Health.

Borg, M. G., Riding, R. J., & Falzon, J. M. (1991). Stress in teaching: A study of occupational stress and its determinants, job satisfaction and career commitment among primary school teachers. *Educational Psychology, 11,* 59–75.

Bowers, A. J., & Sprott, R. (2012). Examining the multiple trajectories associated with dropping out of high school: A growth mixture model analysis. *Journal of Educational Research, 105,* 176–195.

Boyle, G. J., Borg, M. G., Falzon, J. M., Baglioni, J., & Anthony, J. (1995). A structural model of the dimensions of teacher stress. *British Journal of Educational Psychology, 65*(1), 49–67.

CASEL. (2020). *Evidence-based social and emotional learning programs.* https://casel.org/wp-content/uploads/2021/01/11_CASEL-Program-Criteria-Rationale.pdf

Caine, R. N., Caine, G., McClintic, C., & Klimek, K. J. (2015). *12 brain/mind learning principles in action: Teach for the development of higher-order thinking and executive function.* Corwin Press.

Collie, R. J., Shapka, J. D., & Perry, N. E. (2011). Predicting teacher commitment: The impact of school climate and social-emotional learning. *Psychology in the Schools, 48*(10), 1034–1048. doi:10.1002/pits.20611

Collie, R. J., Shapka, J. D., & Perry, N. E. (2012). School climate and social – Emotional learning: Predicting teacher stress, job satisfaction, and teaching efficacy. *Journal of Educational Psychology, 104*(4), 1189–1204. doi:10.1037/a0029356

Cook-Cottone, C. P. (2015). *Mindfulness and yoga for self-regulation: A primer for mental health professionals.* New York: Springer Publishing Company.

Danielson, C., & Chicago Public Schools (CPS). (2011). *CPS framework for teaching companion guide: Version 1.0.* Chicago: CPS.

Duncan, T., Duncan, S., & Strycker, L. (2006). *An introduction to latent variable growth curve modeling: Concepts, issues, and applications*. Mahwah, NJ: Lawrence Erlbaum.

Elias, M. J., Weissberg, R., Dodge, K., Hawkins, J. D., Kendall, P., Jason, L., Perry, C., Rotheram-Borus, M. J., & Zins, J. E. (1994). *The school-based promotion of social competence: Theory, research, action, and policy*. In R. Haggerty, L. Sherrod, N. Garmezy, & M. Rutter (Eds.), Stress, risk, resilience in children and adolescents. (pp. 268–316). New York: Cambridge University Press.

Epstein, J. L., & Sanders, M. G. (2002). Family, school, and community partnerships. In M. H. Bornstein (Ed.), *Handbook of parenting. Practical issues in parenting* (Vol. 5, pp. 407–437). Mahwah, NJ: Lawrence Earlbaum.

Everyday self-care for educators with Chris Soto and Lara Veon. Retrieved from www.routledge.com/Everyday-Self-Care-for-Educators-Tools-and-Strategies-for-Well-Being/Tantillo-Philibert-Soto-Veon/p/book/9780367229825

Fisher, D., Frey, N., & Hattie, J. (2020). *The distance learning playbook, grades K-12: Teaching for engagement and impact in any setting*. Thousand Oaks, CA: Corwin Press.

Goodman, L. (2002). Latent class analysis: The empirical study of latent types, latent variables, and latent structures. In J. Hagennaars & A. McCutcheon (Eds.), *Applied latent class analysis* (pp. 3–55). Cambridge: Cambridge University Press.

Hattie, J. (2009). *Visible learning. Hattie ranking: Influences and effect sizes related to student achievement*. Retrieved September, 28, 2019 from https://visible-learning.org/hattie-ranking-influences-effect-sizes-learning-achievement/

Hattie, J., & Clarke, S. (2018). *Visible learning: Feedback*. London and New York: Routledge.

Herman, K. C., Hickmon-Rosa, J. E., & Reinke, W. M. (2018). Empirically derived profiles of teacher stress, burnout, self-efficacy, and coping and associated student outcomes. *Journal of Positive Behavior Interventions, 20*(2), 90–100.

Howard, S., & Johnson, B. (2004). Resilient teachers: Resisting stress and burnout. *Social Psychology of Education, 7*, 399–420. doi:10.1007/s11218-004-0975-0

Korman, H., O'Keefe, B., & Repka, M. (2020). *Missing in the margins 2020: Estimating the scale of the COVID-19 attendance crisis*. https://bellwethereducation.org/publication/missing-margins-estimating-scale-covid-19-attendance-crisis

Jennings, P. A., & Greenberg, M. T. (2009). The prosocial classroom: Teacher social and emotional competence in relation to student and classroom outcomes. *Review of Educational Research, 79*, 491–525. doi:10.3102/0034654308325693

Kim, K., Kakuyama-Villaber, R., & Gurolnick, A. (2020). *Latent class analysis on sources of work-related stress for teachers and school staff*. Unpublished manuscript. Chapin Hall: University of Chicago.

Kyriacou, C. (2001). Teacher stress: Directions for future research. *Educational Review, 53*, 27–35.

Lips, D. (2020, October 16). *Where the nation's largest school districts stand on reopening.* FreeOpp. Retrieved from https://freopp.org/where-the-nations-largest-school-districts-stand-on-reopening-296d9de2d46c

Lupton, M. J. (1990, July). Singing the black mother: Maya Angelou and autobiographical continuity. In *Black American Literature Forum* (Vol. 24, No. 2, pp. 257–276). St. Louis, MO: St. Louis University.

Milstein, M., & Golaszewski, T. (1985). Effect of organizationally based and individually based stress management efforts in elementary school sittings. *Urban Education, 19*(4), 389–409.

Philibert, C. T. (2021). Everyday SEL in Elementary School: Integrating Social Emotional Learning and Mindfulness Into Your Classroom. Eye on Education.

Philibert, C. T. (2022). Everyday SEL in Middle School: Integrating Social Emotional Learning and Mindfulness Into Your Classroom. Eye on Education.

Ransford, C. R., Greenberg, M. T., Domitrovich, C. E., Small, M., & Jacobson, L. (2009). The role of teachers' psychological experiences and perceptions of curriculum supports the implementation of a social and emotional learning curriculum. *School Psychology Review, 38*(4), 510–532.

Reinke, W. M., Herman, K. C., & Stormont, M. (2013). Classroom-level positive behavior supports in schools implementing SW-PBIS: Identifying areas for enhancement. *Journal of Positive Behavior Interventions, 15*, 39–50.

Roeser, R. W., Schonert-Reichl, K. A., Jha, A., Cullen, M., Wallace, L., Wilensky, R., . . . & Harrison, J. (2013). Mindfulness training and reductions in teacher stress and burnout: Results from two randomized, waitlist-control field trials. *Journal of Educational Psychology, 105*(3), 787.

Roeser, R. W., Skinner, E., Beers, J., & Jennings, P. A. (2012). Mindfulness training and teachers' professional development: An emerging area of research and practice. *Child Development Perspectives, 6*(2), 167–173.

Rosanbalm, K. D., & Murray, D. W. (2017). *Promoting self-regulation in the first five years: A practice brief.* OPRE Brief 2017–79. Administration for Children & Families.

Sarason, S. B. (1990). *The predictable failure of school reform.* San Francisco, CA: Jossey-Bass.

Stoeber, J., & Rennert, D. (2008). Perfectionism in school teachers: Relations with stress appraisals, coping styles, and burnout. *Anxiety, Stress, & Coping, 21*, 37–53.

Travers, C. J., & Cooper, C. L. (1996). *Teachers under pressure: Stress in the teacher profession.* London: Routledge.

Urick, A., & Bowers, A. J. (2014). What are the different types of principals across the United States? A latent class analysis of principal perception of leadership. *Educational Administration Quarterly, 50*(1), 96–134.

Vandenberghe, R., & Huberman, A. M. (1996). *Understanding and preventing teacher burnout: A sourcebook of international research and practice*. Cambridge: Cambridge University Press.

Vega, V. (2012, November 7). *Social and emotional learning research review*. Edutopia. Retrieved from www.edutopia.org/sel-research-learning-outcomes

Walker, T. (2019, October 19). *I didn't know it had a name: Secondary traumatic stress and educators*. National Education Association. Retrieved from www.nea.org/advocating-for-change/new-from-nea/i-didnt-know-it-had-name-secondary-traumatic-stress-and

Wong, H. K. (2009). *Facilitator's handbook: The effective teacher*. Mountain View, CA: HK Wong Publications.

Younghusband, L., Garlie, N., & Church, E. (2003). High school teacher stress in Newfoundland, Canada. Paper presented at *the international conference on education*, Hawaii.